Letters From My Brother

by

Nancy Robison

Copyright © 2008 by Nancy L. Robison

ISBN: Softcover   978-0-6152-1817-5

All rights reserved. No part of this book may be reproduced or transmitted in any form or by any means, electronic or mechanical, including photocopying, recording, or by any information storage and retrieval system, without permission in writing from the copyright owner.

This is a work of non-fiction.

First Printing

This book was printed in the United States of America.

To order additional copies of this book, contact:

Roval Publishing & Digital Services
P.O. Box 822441
N. Richland Hills, TX 76182-2441

1- (888) 485-8830

www.rovalpublishing.net
or
www.rovalpublishing.com

Dedication

For Bob, wherever he is!

Forward

Letters From my Brother, started with a stack of letters saved by my mother and written by her son about his pilot training and experiences serving in the Eighth Air Force during WWII and of the experiences of those of us on the home front. Even though he was twelve years my senior (I was adopted) and I was only a little girl at the time, I had eyes and ears that absorbed everything around me – the sadness when those scary missing-in-action telegrams arrived and worse still the deadly letters from the War Department announcing the death of a serviceman.

This is a story of a boy's life, his love of flying, his girlfriends and those he left behind; of how losing someone can affect your life forever and the lives of those who could not stand the pain and would rather take their own life then live without their loved one.

This is not particularly a happy story, as war is never happy, and it is one that has been lived by many with drama, romance, adventure, mystery, loyalty and patriotism.

Training for these young men took over a year of their life and was a huge job. The demand to remember what they learned in their books and then to execute the exercises in the air; to cope with climate, food, commanding officers, new studies and learning new planes wore heavy on the boys, many who had never been away from home before. And then a large percentage of them were killed on their first flying mission.

The first draft of this story was written fifty years ago when it was still fresh in my mind with the intention of someday writing this book. After 70 published books and 900 plus published stories and articles I feel my experience has helped me to complete this project; - also a lot of the information was gleaned from my brother's descriptive letters, as well as those written by our mother and other relatives.

Portions of this book are found in my memoir – *Does Anybody Want a Little Kewpie?*

Nancy Robison

I With a Song in My Heart

Robert Caulifield Remple was not any different that any of his friends the same age, but to me he was very special. In 1937 when he was fifteen years old and I was three, I was adopted into the family. Being just a teenager he could have ignored me completely, but he didn't. He was always patient, solicitous, and loving to me. He didn't mind at all that I had stepped in on his territory or was becoming a part of his family. He treated me as if I was something special. He was my big brother, handsome and kind.

The night before we went to the courts to make my adoption final, I performed on the stage, at a local school, with other three year olds and sang a song with these words: *"Does anybody want a little kewpie? A little kewpie just like me. I'm left alone, won't someone take me home and cuddle up and love me as there own."* The song was written in honor of the kewpie dolls that were so popular at the time, but the words were very apropos for my situation. My brother didn't actually cuddle me, but he loved me and I loved him.

Bob's passion was anything with a motor. His uncle, Marshall, Mother's brother, bought a 1930 Model "A" Ford, which sat parked under the tall date palms on Cimarron Street in Los Angeles where we lived. And it stayed there without moving for a year until Bob was old enough to drive it. But it didn't stop him and his buddies from sitting in that car for hours pretending they were off on wild adventures. Two sat in the front seat and two in the rumble seat, laughing and telling stories. The four of them, Bob, Dick Jessup, George Hay, and Charles Legrand had their picture taken, posed with arms around each other wearing bell bottom jeans and white starched long sleeve shirts, rolled up at the cuffs. They could have been called the Four Musketeers for they were practically inseparable. Little did they know what the near future had in store for them.

Uncle Marshall worked for Harley Davidson Motorcycle Company and rode beautiful shiny motorcycles over to our house to show Bob. Before Mother could stop him, Bob would climb on behind his uncle and off they would go spinning around corners and riding around and around the block. It wasn't long before Bob had a motorcycle of his own.

Marshall was a bachelor at the time and latched onto Bob as a younger brother. He filled Bob's ears with news of the latest models of cars, motorcycles and airplanes.

The house that we lived in was a duplex on a corner lot of 54th and Cimarron Streets in Los Angeles, but it gave the appearance of a single dwelling from the front. Just inside the front door was a small entrance hall with two doors, each going to one section of the house. We shared a phone with our neighbors through a cut in the wall between the two houses. The front lawn wrapped around the corner going all the way back to an alley. There was a side garden on either side of the house with patios and large fig trees. The duplex shared a common attic which was big enough to hold two beds. It was a nice place to sleep in the summer but not cozy enough for the winter. Bob slept there a lot, pretending he was camping out. An underground bunker with dirt floor and rock sides, used once for a tool shed, was attached to back of the house. This is where Bob spent many hours working with chemistry experiments and building balsa wood model airplanes. Taking particular care with the tissue covering on the wings, he never flew the planes, just hung them by string from the ceiling where they dangled and swung in the breeze. He must have had ten of them in sizes from a small hand to a 30 inch wing span.

Along 54th Street running east and west was a trolley line. Bright yellow and green "street cars," powered by an overhead electric trolley wire ran on tracks in front of the duplex. Lining the side street were rows of very tall date palm trees. Heavy winds sent palm fronds down scattering them across the lawn, in the street and sometimes on the rail track. On the front of each trolley car was a "cow catcher" or a scoop – a shovel type thing that kept the rails cleared of debris. Sometimes boys would put pennies on the track to flatten them. And naughty boys put grease or soap on the track just to watch the wheels spin.

On the back of the lot was a four unit apartment building – two up and two down. Grandmother, Mother's mother, lived in one of them. The apartments faced Cimarron Street and had its own address. The apartments were rented, as well as one side of the duplex providing income for the family. A laundry room with a tub and a washing machine with a hand-wringer was in a separate room in the back just off the alley and used by all tenants. In the alley were metal containers to dump garbage that was picked up daily by trucks. A cement incinerator for burning trash was in the side yard. A schedule was never needed. The compound was like a big family. Everyone worked together to keep harmony.

The ice wagon stopped on our street every couple of days. Not everyone had an electric refrigerator. We had one because Dad worked for a furniture company and got a discount on appliances. But many of our neighbors still had ice boxes that required blocks of ice. We would meet the ice man and get slivers of ice to suck on like Popsicles.

Before Bob learned to drive a car he took flying lessons. Again from the uncle who adored him. Every Saturday morning, Uncle Marshall took Bobby, as he called him, to the Los Angeles Municipal Airport. Small in size with only a few hangers, propeller planes would land and take off without much notice. But off on one runway was a grassy field where the single engine planes, used for lessons, were kept. By age seventeen Bob received his pilot's license. He was smitten. Flying was number one on his list of passions. But a very close second was riding motorcycles.

The world was coming unsettled in 1939. The headlines of the Los Angeles Examiner reported in large letters BRITAIN DECLARES WAR ON GERMANY and the United States was coming slowly out of a depression. (That was one reason I was adopted. My birth parents could hardly feed the five children they already had and wanted me to have a better life, so I was told).

In 1940, President Franklin Delano Roosevelt returned to office for the third term; Dupont replaced nylon for silk in women's stockings, and a helicopter flew for a full fifteen minutes. The world was changing. So was our homelife.

There were still hobos or tramps around in 1940. They walked the alleys looking for food or work. Many times someone knocked on our back door and Mother always found some little thing for them to do – wash windows, rake leaves, clean the yard, carry heavy items from the house to the garage; and instead of paying them money, which she had very little of, she would fix them a hot meal. These were usually nice men, clean and decent, just unfortunate and out of work. I watched while a stranger sat on our back porch eating food off our kitchen dishes. They often had a sad look and I worried that they didn't have a nice home to go to like I did. Maybe someone should adopt them, I thought.

Dad was a top salesman with the Los Angeles Furniture

Company, specializing in oriental rugs, working mostly on commission with a small salary, which was adequate but not quite enough for a growing family. So Mother, seeking a chance for more income, suggested they rent out the duplex where they were living and buy another house up the street. We moved to a one story three bedroom white wood cottage at 1710 Cimarron Street.

The house had a yard with two huge walnut trees that dropped lots of nuts and caused many Blue Jays to squabble over the contents. It was a quiet house with no piano or music, just shadows from the trees that played on the walls in the late afternoon sun and the tick-tock of Grandma's wall clock.

In 1941, Bob got his chance to fly real planes. I remember the day well. Sunday morning, December 7, 1941, I was riding my bike on the sidewalk. It was a quiet, peaceful, ordinary Sunday morning. The air was brisk yet the California sun shone strong and brightened the blue sky. Neighbors were mowing lawns, some were washing cars, radios were playing music from different stations which reached a sound of confusion as I passed from one yard to another. Then quite suddenly all music stopped. And all stations converged into one voice which amplified like a loud speaker down the street. "Pearl Harbor under attack..."

I stopped in my tracks and looked around, knowing something was strange. One neighbor dropped his hose and ran into the house letting water pour into the gutter. Another stopped cutting her roses and dashed into her house, slamming the screen door behind her. Dad, who was mowing our lawn left the mower idle while he ran into the house to gather around the radio with Mother in time to hear the famous words spoken by President Roosevelt, "This day will go down in infamy." I wondered what it was all about.

Bob was just nineteen, a grown man in my eyes, handsome with a slight build, dark hair inherited from his Prussian father and blue eyes from his Irish mother. His main interest at this time was a Harley Davidson motorcycle and a girl named Charlene. His first motorcycle was shiny black with white fenders. It had a leather seat and a kick start. It was a perfect means of transportation and a way of entertainment for him. His friends all got motors too. Tearing the motorcycles apart was something Bob and his buddies liked to do best.

Bob's second Harley was his pride and joy. It was a little bigger, painted a glistening turquoise blue with black leather saddle bags studded with multi-colored stones. Motorcycles were not made for two; however Bob mounted a jump seat or buddy seat in front of the regular seat for carrying a passenger – and that was often me.

Saturday morning's Bob and his buddies turned the backyard into a maintenance shop. They met half way in and half way out of the garage, stripped their bikes down to the frame, removing chains, plugs and what have you. Then after a thorough cleaning in pans of gasoline, they put the parts all back in place and wondered what to do about the left-overs. Then they saddle-soaped the leather saddle bags and seats until they glistened. While they worked, I entertained them. Strutting around in drooping marabou boas, big hats covered with ostrich feathers, beaded gowns and wobbly high-heeled, high-topped buttoned shoes, all from the Victorian trunk belonging to Grandma, I turned and looked over my shoulder, waved the feathered boa and strutted my stuff, while singing, *"Toodle lum a lum a, Toodle lum a lum a, Toodle ay a. Any umbrellas, any umbrellas to sell today?"* Bob's friends hooted and hollered, cheered and clapped for more. So how could I resist? They were a good audience and I loved it. Bob's buddies were my friends too. They treated me like a little sister. I looked forward to those Saturday mornings.

On Sunday mornings Bob would take off for the beach or the mountains. Affixing clear riding goggles over his eyes, accelerating the gas by the throttle on the right handle grip, he kicked up the stand and roared down the driveway with a girlfriend clinging to his back like an Indian papoose. Her job was to provide a picnic lunch. Meeting with his buddies by a stream they ate and joked and just plain loved life and being together.

When he started college, I started kindergarten. Taking a few classes at UCLA, Bob also had a part time job with Joseff's of Hollywood, using his artistic talent for designing jewelry for the movies. Art and drafting classes in High School taught him precision in design work.

On that particular Sunday morning, the 7th of December 1941, Bob roared up the grass driveway, turned off the motor, leaned his "bike" on the kick stand, and sprinted up the four wooden back steps into the house. He clopped through the kitchen, across the linoleum floor with his heavy black leather riding boots. Quietly he removed his black leather gloves as he crept up behind his mother who stood leaning against a pillar separating dining and living rooms. Jamming his gloves into the rear pocket of his jeans, he leaned on the mahogany dining table, crossing his arms across his chest as he listened to the news report that was repeated over and over again.

He looked at his mother. Her head was bent, her eyes watered as she bit down hard on her lower lip to prevent the tears from flowing. She took a lace trimmed handkerchief from the pocket of her cotton print house dress and dabbed at her eyes before she looked at her son. They did not speak. There was a bond between them that only they felt but others could see.

Dad sat down deep in the feather-filled cushioned chair next to the radio where he liked to listen to the base ball games on the weekends; and to Jack Benny; Amos and Andy and Fibber McGee and Molly during the week. As the news told of the disaster at Pearl Harbor, Dad had both hands covering his face to hide the tears that were flowing.

My brother said in a tranquil tone, "Mom, Dad, I've heard the news." He reached over and turned down the volume on the radio, then continued. "I don't want to shock you. I know you've had enough shocking news already, but I'm going to enlist."

His parents looked at him with tear filled eyes. His mother covered her mouth with her hand, while his father just shook his head and blew his nose. And I stood by watching and wondering, with my seven year old eyes and ears, what it was all about. What and where was Pearl Harbor? And why was it under attack and by whom?

Bob tried to calm his parent's fears. He knew his parents well. Better probably than they knew him. Already prepared to reason with them he said, "We all know what a dreadful thing war is but you have to admit it was not totally a surprise. I've listened to you talk about the war in Europe and now it's practically in our front yard."

They nodded, still in shock, still not saying anything.

Bob continued, "The guys have been discussing what we would do if it ever came about, now it has and you know I am extremely eligible for duty. If I don't enlist, I'll get drafted. And if I'm drafted there is no choice of services and I want to fly! I'm signing up for the Air Corps along with Jack Alexander and some of the others."

Mother pulled a dining room chair away from the table and sat on it. "We're proud of you, son," she sniffed.

Dad pushed himself up out of the deep-cushioned chair, wiped his nose again and crossed over to Bob. He patted him on the back but could not find voice to speak. Bob held out his hand and gripped the hand of his father. The two men stood motionless but with a firm grip.

Finally choking out some words, his dad said, "The way you know motors, I'm sure the Air Corps will welcome you."

"I'll have to admit," Bob said, now smiling, "I'm going to miss that beauty of a bike, but I'm not going to sell it right away. If it's all right with you, Pop, I'd like to leave it in the garage."

Once again his dad found his throat cut off with emotion. He could not speak but he nodded his approval then left the room.

His mom looked at him with soul-filled eyes. "I should have guessed you wouldn't have flying out of your head. I believe someday you will have your own airfield and you'll ride out to your private plane on your motorcycle."

Bob smiled, his blue eyes reflected the afternoon light that streamed through the open window as he gazed through the sheer organdy curtains into the cloudless sky. "I've missed flying," he said. "The flying club we had in high school was a wonderful opportunity for me. The Gliders and Piper Cubs would hardly be classified as a plane now, but I sure had fun in those flying machines and they gave me a good start."

Mom's expression softened and she knew that Bob loved flying so much that no matter how much she tried to discourage the idea it would be useless. His confidence removed any pessimistic thought she might have. She left the room leaving Bob alone with his thoughts.

II Don't Sit Under the Apple Tree
With Anyone Else But Me

Bob's acceptance letter into the Air Corps arrived with the time, date and place of where to report. He was not yet twenty. (Now that I have 20 year old grandsons, I see how very young that was).

Only the day before departure was the date his mom and dad had clandestinely planned a surprise going away party for him. Bob spent the entire morning and part of the afternoon cleaning his motorcycle. His hands were covered with grease and his finger nails were black with crank case oil. He had removed each moving and non-moving part of the machine, soaked it in the proper lubricate then reassembled it, except for the tires which were rolled away to a dark corner of the double garage.

While he worked I entertained him as I had done so many times before. Most of the dresses hung on me like beaded sacks, but Bob said he liked watching the fashion show I put on. I had a soft spot in my heart for that turquoise motorcycle too. On dancing school days, Bob sat on the small jump seat and put me behind him on the big seat. Together we would roar up Slauson Avenue, me with arms wrapped around his waist and face buried in his black leather jacket, the smell of leather delighting me. He would drop me off McKinney's Dance Studio and pick me up an hour later. How proud I was to show off that I could ride on a motorcycle behind my big brother.

The machine glistened as it sat propped up on braces as Bob polished the multicolored stones set in silver mountings that surrounded the black leather saddle bags. He flipped the chamois cloth around the fenders and carefully sponged up every drop of moisture.

Mother came out the back door and down the steps carrying a glass of lemonade. She called to him and he looked up. "Oh, is that for me?" He took the glass and in one motion placed it to his mouth, tipped his head back and gulped down the refreshing drink.

Placing the glass down on the cement, he continued flipping the chamois cloth around the fenders like a shoe shine boy working for a big tip. He wore only an undershirt with his jeans and to me he looked very muscular. "Do you have any plans for this evening?" she asked.

"Nothing special," he answered. Just recently he had broken up with Charlene, or she broke up with him. She was a super nice girl and they went together all through high school. She reminded me of a gardenia or a camellia flower. I don't know why except that she had a round face and very white skin, and always smelled sweet. Charlene was a quiet girl, not shy but polite and very nice to me. She wore red lipstick on her full lips and tended toward conservative dress, mostly white blouses and blue or black slacks and a snood to cover her chestnut colored hair when she went riding with Bob on his motorcycle.

Sometimes she would come over on Sunday afternoons, after their long motorcycle rides, and we would make fudge from the recipe on the Hershey's cocoa box. Because it took a lot of stirring, they let me help. After the fudge was poured into a plate to cool I got to lick the pan clean. So now he was without a girlfriend and looking forward to going away for goodness knows how long. I felt sad for him and already I missed Charlene. "I thought I would give some of the guys a call and see if we could get together as a little farewell," he told his mother.

Mother tried to avert her eyes and not give away that she was hiding something. "Your father and I were hoping you would have dinner with us."

"Gee whiz," Bob said, using a favorite expression of his, "I'd like to Mom, but you know how it is? I won't be seeing the guys for a long time and....." He saw her hurt expression. "I don't mean that I don't want to be with you," he fumbled.

She smiled and nodded understandingly. She was aware of how her son felt about his friends but she also knew that he wouldn't find any of them at home that night as she had personally gone through his phone book, when he was not looking, and made sure everyone in it was invited to the surprise party.

Finishing up with the last stroke, putting the motorcycle up on jacks and covering it with canvas, he had me put away my costumes, close the lid of the trunk and follow him out of the garage. Then he pulled the side doors of the garage together and closed them on his prize possession, then catapulted over the back stair railing, bounded into the kitchen, slid onto the stool next to the phone and took the phone book from his back pocket and started dialing numbers.

Flipping through page after page and finding no one home or the same answer from those who were, "Sorry old man, like to see you tonight but I've made other plans." Disappointed he slammed down the phone and yelled from the kitchen, "Hey, Pop, can I use the car for about an hour?"

Dad was in a dilemma. He didn't want to give away the surprise so he said that he could use it but, "Don't stay away too long."

Bob grabbed the leather case of keys off the kitchen table and bounded out the back door. He slid behind the wheel of the maroon colored 1940 Chevrolet Coupe, (a car Dad had bought off the showroom floor for $500 especially with Bob in mind) and backed out the driveway. Through the front window I watched him go, and then looked at Mom and Dad.

"Now where do you suppose he's off to?" Dad asked.

Mother shrugged. "No telling, but he'll be back before long."

"How can you be so sure? We have reservations at Bit O' Sweden on the Sunset Strip and all those people coming."

"Don't worry," she said with confidence. "He won't find anyone to pal around with tonight because I made sure everyone was invited to the party."

"Are you sure you didn't forget anyone?"

"I'm sure," she said. "That is, I hope so. If I've forgotten even one person, we're sunk!" Then reassuring herself she said, "No, I'm sure of it. I haven't forgotten anyone."

I wanted to say that she had forgotten me. Why wasn't I included in the celebration? Someone said I was too young. Grandma, who was my baby-sitter, explained that if I went then my two little cousins would have to be invited too and they were not very well behaved.

Afternoon shadows lengthened as the sun hid behind the row of white framed houses across the street. Dad paced back and forth across the living room rug while Mother dressed in her brown velvet with crystal beads. Her brown hair was set in deep waves that touched the temples of her brow.

"Are you sure he will fall for this surprise party idea?" Dad asked.

"Well it stands to reason," She answered, "if none of his friends are available, he'll have no other choice than to go with us." Reaching in the closet she grabbed a blue tie and thrust it at him. "Here, wear this one. It matches your blue suit better than that brown one."

Changing ties while alternating glances in the mirror and out the window, he was almost finished when the car pulled into the driveway. To show they were not really concerned, Mother and Dad quickly grabbed seats in the living room. I picked up my doll and changed her dress. Dad turned the radio on but was not listening to it. He looked across the room at Mother who sat on the heavy over-stuffed couch filing her nails. The last rays of sunshine filtered through the front window and formed a geometric pattern across the Oriental rug. Mom reached over to the side table and pulled the chain on the bulky pottery based lamp. The fringe on the shade quivered when she brushed by it with her hand.

A frown formed across Dad's brow as he looked around the room. All the furnishings had come from the store where he was employed. A job he was not particularly fond of, but what else could he do? Raised on a farm in Nebraska he had barely finished fourth grade. How he and Mother ever got together we have no record of knowing. Mother was once a nurse and he could have been a patient. Who knows? In her twenties she was very trim and petite and he was strong and muscular. There must have been a physical attraction between them. It didn't bother Mother, I guess, that he was older by fifteen years and had been married before with two daughters somewhere in Texas. They were married by a Justice of the Peace in 1920. Every few seconds Dad lit a cigarette and puffed on it nervously, flicking ashes into the ash tray.

Finally in entered a downcast, pensive young man, sauntering into the room. "If it's all right I'd like to have dinner with you tonight. All my friends are busy. What a sorry thing and on my last night too!" He sounded so dejected it would be hard not to feel sorry for him.

"We'd be delighted," Mother said. "Now hurry and get dressed. We're ready to go."

"I'm ready," he said.

Mother grinned and shook her head. "No, dear. Your dark pinstripe will do very nicely." He looked at his mother in her best dress, his father in a dark blue suit.

Before he walked away he said, "Why is everyone so fickle? I thought Charlene and I had an understanding. I mean we've broken up sort of - but she could at least wait until I'm gone before she goes out on me. Here it is my last night home, I may never see her again and she doesn't even want to go out with me one last time!"

Mother ached inside wanting to comfort her son, to let him know the reason for everything. If only he knew how much all his friends really did like him. They'd all be there to wish him well.

A frown creasing his brow, Bob went on, "She's probably sore because I joined up but that's no excuse for my buddies. Every one of them has a date tonight including my girl, or who I thought was my girl!" He scuffed off to his room.

I trailed behind and watched him from the doorway. Bob did not look like his usual happy self. In fact, I had never seen him so sad. Slowly and deliberately he hung the black leather jacket on a hanger and shoved it far into the back of the closet. The knee high riding boots he stuffed with wadded up newspaper and placed them out of reach in the dark recesses of the closet under the jacket. The faded jeans fell to the floor. He scooped them up with his foot and shoved them into the clothes hamper. Leisurely he showered and dressed while Dad paced the floor watching the time and Mom tried to calm his impatience.

Finally dressed in a suit and tie, he asked if he could drive. Much to Dad's dismay, he handed over the keys. (As I was not present at the rest of the evening I can only record what was told to me later and I lived every minute as if I were there).

Bob drove as leisurely as he had dressed. Dad tried to hasten him but whenever he suggested driving faster, Bob only wanted to know, "What's the hurry?"

Mother could only think of the thirty people waiting for the guest of honor to arrive.

Bob didn't ask where they were going, nor did he talk much on the way. It was as if he was in another world, thinking about something else, perhaps feeling a little sorry for himself. Following directions automatically he didn't question nor seemed impressed when they stopped in front of the very fine Bit O' Sweden restaurant. "Isn't this a little fancy for a family meal?" he asked, coming out of his lethargy.

"Since it is your last night home, we thought you might enjoy a nice restaurant," Mother told him. "After all this is not the night to eat at the car barns!"

Dad was quick to defend his favorite place to eat. "There's absolutely nothing wrong with eating at the car barns. All the streetcar conductors eat there and the food is good!" Located in the yard where the trolley cars were housed or barned, the café was frequented by the conductors and local people who liked plain food. Not a pretty place, but good for home style cooking.

It was not Mother's favorite place but she realized the touchiness of the subject and decided this was not the time to discuss the choice of eating establishments. "I admit that it has good food," she replied, "but none of us are streetcar conductors and besides the scenery is nicer here."

They waited at the top of the stairs for the Maitre D' Hotel who escorted them to the Banquet Room. The doors were flung open, the Maitre D' stepped back and there before Bob was a room full of familiar faces. All of his friends that were too busy to say good-bye sat before him smiling and cheering, "Surprise!"

Bob's lower jaw dropped open. The color drained from his face and it looked as if he might faint. His mom and dad stood on either side of him and guided him to the head table where a cake decorated with tiny American flags and a red air plane sat before him. Suddenly the color returned to his face and he turned as red as the airplane. He could not find his voice but he had not lost his senses. Across the room sat a beautiful girl in a blue feathered hat, her eyes closed with laughter. She was someone he had met only a few weeks ago and added her number to his phone book. Now here she sat, clapping and smiling at him.

In that entire room of people, he focused only on one. He stood and walked over to her. The feathers on her hat were like a cloud of blue fluff that drifted around her head like a halo. He took her gloved hand and led the way back to his table and seated her next to him.

"And what about Charlene?" I interrupted the telling of the story.

"She couldn't make it," Mother answered, "And probably just as well. Bob was in love. It showed all over his face."

Mom and Dad congratulated themselves on a well-planned and complete surprise party. Dinner was served and everyone began to eat except Bob. When his dad noticed his plate was untouched, he whispered to him, "You really should try to eat. It's quite good and better than what you will be getting in the service."

Leaning back on his chair, he whispered back to his dad, "I have a confession to make. You see, I stopped at the Witch Stand Drive-In this afternoon and had a malt and a hamburger. So, I'm not hungry. And truthfully, I don't think it would stay down now anyway."

III This is the Army Mr. Jones

The following morning Bob was happy, excited and felt great, but he couldn't eat anything. He was to leave by bus from the induction center, in downtown Los Angeles, and was headed for basic training. We piled into the Chevy coupe; Bob and Dad in the front and Mother and I in the small back seat. At the terminal he jumped out of the car, gave us a big reassuring smile, grabbed his small bag and rushed to the waiting bus. Now it was my time to be sad. When would we see him again? What would we do without him?

Then she showed up. I didn't know who she was but Dad suddenly turned into Prince Charming. He couldn't say enough flattering things to her like how nice she looked so early in the morning. No wonder he was a top salesman! She wore a pink crepe dress. At the neck was a black and white cameo pin. She had skin so white it looked as if she'd never seen the sun. It was obvious Dad adored her. When she rolled her big brown eyes Dad would make some flirty remark that made her laugh. Then he laughed too as if he were twenty years old.

Along with hundreds of other boys, Bob boarded one of the buses and sat next to an open window. He smiled and waved to us, but had a different look for the girl with the paprika colored hair that glowed in the morning light like an orange ball of fire. Who was she? He leaned out the window and yelled, "I'll let you know my address if you promise to write."

"You bet I will!" she answered with a big smile showing her perfect row of white teeth. "I will!"

Bob took the small red plane from his pocket that had been on the cake the night of the party and hung it out the bus window. The wind caught hold of the tiny propeller and whizzed it around. "Will you keep this for me?"

She walked towards the bus as he tossed the plane out. She caught it and clutched it to her breast as his bus pulled away.

Dad put his arms around Mother and the girl and walked

them back to our car (she had arrived by taxi) parked by the curb, chattering all the way about the fun party and what a surprise it was for Bob. Something he would always remember. I followed behind and then I knew who she was....the girl in the blue feathered hat! The one my brother was in love with. For the first time in my young life, I saw the green dragon – that awful beast of jealousy.

What had happened to Charlene, Bob's girlfriend that I was used to? In my innocence I truly believed they would get back together and now he was two-timing her for the girl in the blue feathered hat. Didn't he know what he was doing? But Mom and Dad really liked this person and I would have to like her too, at least for Bob's sake.

Her name was Dorothy Barbara Swinger and quite a pretty girl with a big smile and sparkling eyes. She wore her hair in a pompadour in front off her forehead and with a long page-boy to her shoulders down the back, as was the style in 1942. Her fingers were long and slender and she wore red nail polish to match her candy apple red lipstick. She worked in a dress shop in Hollywood – coincidentally enough called NANCY'S.

From the first morning that we met her, she became an important part of this story. She lived with her divorced mother in a small stucco duplex near the Coliseum in Los Angeles. She had two brothers who lived in Utah, presumably with their father, although no one spoke much of the mysterious Mr. Swinger.

Mother and Dad fell in love with Dorothy Barbara immediately. Mother especially embraced the girl in her heart and they became very good friends, and in the future they would be sharing letters and information from Bob.

Bob became an Air Corps Cadet and was sent to ground school at the Santa Ana Army Air Corp Base (SAAAB) located mid way between the sleepy towns of Costa Mesa and Santa Ana in the County of Orange, about 50 miles south of Los Angeles. Nearby was the Orange County airport where only the Commanding Officers kept their planes. Nothing over the size of a P-38 was permitted to be parked there. Two blimp hangers 17 stories high were located in nearby Santa Ana. This was a 1300 acre camp specializing in ground training, which included studies in chemical warfare, defense, code, cryptography, military customs and courtesies, ground forces, air forces, maps and charts, physics, mathematics and so forth. Bob would receive his pre-flight training here where cadets would be divided into squadrons and classified as pilots, bombardiers, navigators or whatever.

Anxious moments were spent waiting for letters or phone calls from Bob. In his first letter home, he drew a picture of a young soldier, sitting on a short stool in a much too small Army uniform, enormous boots, a hat that had fallen over his ears and tears flowing from his eyes as he peeled a bucket full of onions. The return address was:

A/C Robert C. Remple
Squadron 1D
1st CLFSN, Wing
S.A.A.B
Santa Ana, Calif.

The letter head was the emblem of a cadet – a pair of wings with United States Army Air Corps printed under it.

Artistically printed in his hand with perfectly spaced letters, it said:

July 29, 1942
"Dear Mother and Dad,
This morning we started to take our test which will classify us as pilots, bombardiers, and navigators.

They are still pretty easy with us, but we have to get up at 5:30 just the same. Breakfast is at 6:30 or sometimes 6:00.

The first night I arrived I was issued a "zute suit". It was about 3 inches to short and fit very tight around my ankles. But then I looked up Blackie (a friend) and found out that he is in charge of a supply room. He gave me a "suit" that fit a little bit better. He is leaving this Thursday. Today we were issued mechanics caps which was very much needed. I had to have something to cover my - what's left of the - hair on my head. It is practically a shave!

I am expecting to see you Sunday at 9:00. I'll phone you and tell you where to meet me.

They are still stuffing us with food. Breakfast – oatmeal, eggs and bacon, prunes, orange juice, milk, bread. Lunch – corned beef and cabbage, lettuce with dressing, potatoes, carrots and turnips, apricot pudding, fig bars, milk. Dinner – leg of lamb with dressing, French fried potatoes, lettuce and tomato salad, string beans, milk and punch, fresh strawberries and ice cream. (<u>Unlimited</u> supply of <u>everything</u>).

Excuse my writing because I am lying down on my cot.

No one has received any mail in our squad yet. I guess it is tied up some place.

Love, Bob"

Of course Mom had written to him the moment he left and every day since; so had Dorothy Barbara.

Sunday was visiting day. Dorothy Barbara sat in the back seat of the tiny Chevrolet Coupe with me where we inhaled smoke from Dad's Lucky Strike cigarettes and tried to get him to open the windows. We drove the 50 miles to Orange County at a top speed of 35 mph, past Knott's Berry Farm, through Fullerton, past the blimp house where they stored the Goodyear Blimp until finally we came to a tree-lined street and the Baker Street entrance of the base. A handsome young man in uniform smiled at us at the gate, directed us where to park and we had arrived.

It was nice to get out of the car and stretch but it was a hot muggy day and not too pleasant. The base was dry and so were our throats. Even though the training center had been formed before the outbreak of war, there were many more recruits than expected. Barracks were finished in a hurry and tents were put up to hold the overflow. Everywhere we looked were young men dressed in brown. They blended in with the dry brown ground. Dad said, "They all look the same to me. Same uniforms, same hats, like a thousand twins."

Bob had been waiting for us and ran to the car. Dorothy Barbara shouted, "There he is," and scrambled out of the car pushing the back of the front seat forward squeezing Mother into the dash board. They ran into each other's arms and he swung her around like long lost lovers. Dad parked the car and we got out. The happy couple walked hand and hand over to us. They could hardly take their eyes off each other long enough to say hello.

Dad was emotional and choked back his tears. "Where are the planes?" he asked.

"We aren't flying yet, Pop. This is just the preliminary of all preliminaries. It's here that we get tested and divided into pilots, radio operators or ground crew. Keep your fingers crossed that I make it. I really don't want to stay on the ground! Come on, I'll show you around the circus."

Bees swarmed around a red Coca Cola machine that sat outside the service center building. Bob put a coin in the machine and it belched out a bottle of dark liquid. Passing it to me first, I took a sip. WARM! Yuk! I spit it out. It tasted terrible. Bob apologized saying that the machine must be out of ice and placed the bottle in the open crate.

We continued the tour with Bob pointing out the barracks,

the mess hall, the PX and the parade ground. "Other than that there isn't much else to see around here except dust," he said. "So, let's get out of the sun." He held the door open to the service center and we looked for seats, but had to be grateful for standing room. It wasn't long before he was called to the parade grounds and we found seats in the stands.

The parade grounds were filled with aviation cadets. Each squadron had 180 persons. Four or five squadrons formed a group and two groups made a wing.

It was difficult to pick Bob out of the crowd. All were dressed in class "A" (dress) uniforms. They passed by the reviewing stand to a March played by the Base Band. At the command, "Eyes right!" all heads snapped to the right and arms shot up in a salute. And there was dust everywhere. It was impossible to single out any one in particular in the sea of khaki.

Dad was busting his buttons with pride. Mother's blue straw hat was tipped to one side, her hands folded in her lap and her eyes riveted on the parade grounds. Dorothy Barbara wore her best smile in case Bob looked our way. We were all hot and sticky together and it didn't matter a bit. There was something very thrilling about seeing all the men marching in straight lines, arms swinging the same way, heads turning simultaneously.

Bob told us a little story about how they kept the lines straight. Clutched in the hands of each cadet was a penny to remind him not to swing his arms more than 6 inches in front and 3 inches in back. When the penny flew out of the hand, it meant you were swinging too much. Then after passing the reviewing stand, everyone tossed their penny over their right shoulder for luck. "One day some smart guy collected all the pennies on the parade ground and found enough to buy a war bond!" he told us with a smile. True or not it made a good story.

The parade over, Bob found us again and the day was over much too soon.

At the car we said our farewells. Mother handed over the box of cookies that she had made and then discreetly climbed into the backseat of the car and waited for Bob and Dorothy Barbara to say their good-byes. Their embrace and kiss was light and tender but from the heart. Bob looked as if he might cry. "Write to me," he said.

Mother said of course she would and D.B. gave him a huge smile and wave as she climbed into the front seat next to Dad. From there she blew him a kiss. The wind from the day had mussed her hair and she tried to brush it back from her face, then gave up and stuck her head out the window waving to him until we were out of sight.

They probably thought I was asleep on the way home because they were talking as if Dorathy Barbara was already a part of the family telling her stories about Bob as a young boy; when he was arrested for shooting out store windows with his uncle's B-B gun, and of course about the Model "A" Ford that he tore apart and reassembled over and over before he was old enough to drive it.

The Chevrolet Coupe hustled along. Dad smiled, relaxed his grip on the steering wheel and let the car drive itself. "You know how we feel about you," Mother said. And Dad made a remark in favor of Dorathy Barbara by saying that Bob "really knows how to pick 'um!" Dorathy Barbara was adored. There was no doubt about that. Whether I was jealous of all the attention she was getting or we just didn't have the right chemistry together, I don't know. But try as I did to make her adorable in my eyes, I just couldn't do it. But my brother loved her and so I must try to do the same.

IV Praise the Lord and Pass the Ammunition

Fuel and food rationing went into affect so fast it was as if this war had been pre-planned by Washington. Enemy control of the high seas reduced the import of sugar, coffee, rubber. Even toilet paper was hard to get. Meat, dairy products, canned goods and paper goods were needed to take care of the troops who were fighting for our country. Not many left on the home front complained. It was their patriotic duty to support the war effort; and whatever they could do to help they did.

War ration book No, 1 had 28 stamps good for sugar, meat, butter, eggs, canned goods and even for shoes. Each stamp had a letter of the alphabet and a number. The number represented the number of points. The letter was for the time period the stamp was valid. If you missed the time, too bad, the stamp could no longer be used.

The OPA (Office of Price Administration) set the price control. A large can of peaches cost 21 cents and it took 21 ration points to buy it. A can of Niblet's corn was 10 cents and took 8 points to buy. Some ration stamps were more precious than money. And it took a lot of figuring before shopping to know what you could get or not get. Then after writing the list and making careful plans it was off to the market only to learn they were out of the products. "But we can offer you this substitute," the grocer would say.

Coffee was rationed too. One pound of coffee was issued every five weeks. That was one cup a day. This was never enough for Dad who enjoyed a cup of coffee and a cigarette several times a day.

Local cafes and restaurants had problems getting food and when they did the prices were very high. A full turkey dinner with all the trimmings was $1.59. A steak dinner was $1.75. But just try and get the meat! Our dear bakery – Saline's - that made such heavenly morning rolls could not get sugar and had to cut back. Jergins' Market - a Mom and Pop store - made big adjustments. And Joes' shoe repair got more business than ever, only he had trouble getting leather to make the repairs on the soles of shoes.

Another ration book was needed for gasoline. Each car had a sticker placed in the lower right hand corner of the front windshield signifying the amount of allotted gasoline per week. The "A" sticker was white on a black back ground and was placed in the lower right hand corner of the windshield. This is what most family cars had. The "B" sticker was green and the "C" was red. These were for commercial vehicles like taxis and trucks. The A coupon book had 32 stamps. Each stamp was exchanged for 4 gallons of gasoline. This was supposed to last one week.

Scrap drives were launched around the country. One pound of waste fat from cooking contained enough glycerin to make one pound of explosives. Mother saved fat in empty tin cans and turned them in at the butcher shop.

Scrap metal was recycled to make hand grenades, they said. Everyone got into the act giving up their metal rakes and tools and felt a great deal of patriotism. Everyone wanted to participate in helping the war effort. With wagon pulled behind us, I went with my neighborhood kids to collect used tires, tin cans, newspapers and anything for the scrap drive. Then we would unload at the vacant lot on the corner where it was collected for recycling.

Bob was a conscientious, serious, determined student. He desired to become a qualified pilot. Nothing else would do. Although his time was mostly occupied with studies, he still found time to write home.

The day finally arrived – the day that Bob was waiting for. The anxiety was overwhelming. Would he pass? Did he make it? Would he qualify to fly or would he remain unhappily on the ground? The news was out. Along with the crowd he rushed to the bulletin board to find his name. He had made it. He had been selected for pilot training. He shook hands with his fellow graduates and they discussed with enthusiastic relief and with gratitude their meeting again when transferred to the next step – elementary flying school. Bob phone home with the good news.

"I've got a 48 hours pass. I'll be there tomorrow morning. One of the fellows has a car and will drop me off."

It was as exciting as Christmas. Bob was coming home. Mother got out her rationing book and checked her stamps for meat, sugar and other items and went across the street to Jergins' Market. The neat little store was divided into three sections; each section was managed by an individual; the meat department, the produce and the groceries. Mr. and Mrs. Jergins were the owners. They were both amply built and they both had red hair! When ordering wigs they obviously ordered two of the same style and color. They looked like man and wife twins!

Mr. Kajima, his wife and two daughters managed the produce department. One of the daughters was close to my age and became my friend. The butcher, Mr. Muller was a huge man with a suspicious look. Mother was sure he ran a black market ring. Mother being the patriotic person she was always stood firm and condemned those that hoarded and those that would stoop to black marketing.

The meat counter was empty except for a small mound of ground meat heavily decorated with parsley. Disappointed, she asked, "Is this it?"

The butcher answered, "I had some T-bones but they went fast. But I know where you get a nice pot roast for a price," he whispered leaning over the counter.

The sweeter you were to the butcher the better cuts of meat he would save for you. Mother was not about to kiss-up to anyone for any reason. She didn't like Mr. Muller very much and suspected him of cheating. "I don't want to bother with coupons today," he would say, "Just pay the price."

"No thanks," she said. She knew he put his thumb on the scale when weighing the meat and added water to chickens to make them weigh more. "Give me a pound and a half of that." She pointed to the ground meat.

Mr. Muller shrugged, weighed the meat, wrapped and sealed the package, accepted her ration stamps and money and nodded.

Mr. Kajima, the utmost in politeness bowed slightly and asked if he could be of service. In the past Mother had given small gifts of hair ribbons or candy to Mr. Kajima's two daughters. They were a clean, friendly and well dressed Japanese family. Sometimes I would stay after shopping and play with the girls who lived in the small room behind the store. A flimsy curtain hung across the opening that led to a room they called home. Sawdust took the place of rugs. It wasn't a very nice place. There were two cots and two mats for sleeping. Janie and her little sister used the cots. Their parents slept on mats on the cold cement floor. Orange crates were used for chairs. One wobbly table and two old kitchen chairs were in the middle of the room. The table looked as if it had once been used to chop meat. The rest of the room was filled with empty cartons and crates that were used to hold fruits and vegetables. This is where we sat when Janie taught me to read Japanese characters from the Japanese paper. This was intriguing to me because we read it backwards – from the bottom upwards. I learned how to identify "man" and "child" in Japanese characters. In return for their kindness I always took Janie and her little sister a lollipop or something sweet.

On the day that we were getting ready for Bob to come home on leave, Mother replied to Mr. Kajima, "Yes, my son is coming home on leave from the Air Corps and I'm making him a nice dinner." She looked into his dark slanted eyes and was thinking in her heart that perhaps she should not have mentioned anything about the war; after all the Japanese had bombed Pearl Harbor only a few months before. "I'd like a bunch of carrots," she said, "and a head of lettuce."

Early the next morning she began preparation for Bob's homecoming. She mixed the ground meat with bread crumbs, chopped onions, celery and spices, placed the mixture into a loaf pan and placed it in the ice box. Next she put together a chocolate cake.

Dad was up, dressed and breakfasted before the neighborhood rooster could crow. He occupied his time with a few minute jobs and then announced he was going to the corner to wait for Bob's arrival. And there he stood on the cement curb smoking cigarette after cigarette. Looking up the street one direction, then another, he crossed over and searched for a glimpse of an oncoming car of which there were none. It was so early in the morning that none of the neighbors had started their lawn work or car washing. People were still sleeping.

Time passed. The morning sun climbed higher over the roof tops, but still no Bob. Dad walked back and forth, lighting one cigarette after another. Finally a car made its way up the street. He stamped out the cigarette butt and prepared to greet his son. His heart beat quickened with anxiety. But the black and white sedan that pulled up was not the car he was expecting. Nor was the black uniform quite what he was prepared for.

"Good morning, sir," the officer said climbing out of the car. May I ask why you are standing here all morning?"

"Certainly," Dad answered proudly, "My son is coming home today. He's a cadet in the Air Corps, you know. This is his first leave and I'm waiting for him. He said he was getting a ride home with another soldier. I've been standing here so long, I think I've made a hole in the City's sidewalk. Is that why you stopped?"

The police officer shook his head, then walked over to the patrol car and spoke to the other officer behind the wheel. Then to

Dad he said, "You have been reported as a 'peeper'."

"A 'peeper'? There's no one around here to peep at. I'm simply waiting for my boy!" Dad was astounded. "Come to think of it, Mrs. Brody probably turned in the complaint. She lives by herself over there." He pointed to the dilapidated, very much in need of paint, stucco house on the alley. Shrubbery covered the front of it almost entirely except for one small window where a mass of bougainvillea intertwined with English Ivy, covered the doorway. The front lawn was brown with devil grass and dotted with yellowed newspapers that had been neglected. "The neighbors around here feel that she's not all there in her head, if you know what I mean?"

"Sure do, Mister. We get calls from them all day. Sorry to have bothered you. Hope your son gets home soon." The officer went away mumbling, "How could anyone peep into a house like that anyway without being right under the window!"

Dad scuffed the pile of cigarettes he had created into the gutter and started back towards the house. Depressed because he wished to greet his son and deprived of the pleasure, yet concerned that he had not shown up yet, he glanced around one last time. And there coming in the opposite direction was a young man in a brown uniform carrying an overnight bag. He recognized the walk – the quick pace, the shoulders swinging from side to side. Oh, joy! It was Bob! Dad ran to meet him, threw his arms about the boy's shoulders and slapped him softly on the back. "You're home!"

"Sorry I'm late, Pop. We had to drop off some other fellas."

Dad took his bag and they walked up the front cement steps and porch and through the white door. Dad called out, "He's home!"

Mom ran from the kitchen wiping her hands on her apron, then with arms outstretched hugged her boy. Bob picked up his mother and twirled her around. He did the same to me. "Oh, you're getting too big." He said. I laughed. I loved him too.

The kitchen was warm and fragrant from the cake baking inside the oven.

"I smell chocolate cake!" he said.

He had graduated and received his cadet wings and was looking forward to flying. His present to me was a set of gold wings, with a silver propeller in the center, a smaller version of the ones on his cap.

Mom took him in the kitchen where she presented him with a double layer cake, with milk chocolate frosting. He didn't have to beg for a piece. She happily gave him a slice with a glass of milk and then told him all the family news. Bob was polite but it was obvious his thoughts were elsewhere. As soon as the last crumb from his plate was gone, he dashed for the telephone.

Knowing what he was up to, and wanting to see more of him, she said, "Ask her for dinner. It's only meatloaf but with your charm I'm sure it will taste like steak!"

"And how did you know who I was going to call?" he shouted over his shoulder.

"Mothers have a way of knowing," she answered.

In his room, Bob slipped out of the khakis and into the faded blue Levis. Out of the coarse wool jacket, into the cold black leather, out of the brown oxfords, into the knee high riding boots, he transformed his image. Then he went out to the garage and opened the door. He smiled at the sight of the beautiful motorcycle that sat on wooden blocks. I heard him say, "Well, old buddy, the time has come for you and I to part and go our separate ways." He began replacing the tires, then out from behind Grandma's trunk strolled the gray and white cat, that he called "Kitty". (I brought the cat home from a neighbors when she was only a few weeks old, but I didn't take to her as much as my brother did. I named her Twinkletoes – he called her Kitty). She stretched her front paws and then her back ones, yawned and tucking her tail beneath, sat down.

"Well, there you are you old cat," he said.

The cat looked startled then dashed to him and began rubbing herself back and forth across the familiar boots.

"There, there, old cat," he said stroking the fur, "I've missed you too."

The cat purred. Bob stooped over and scratched her under the chin and sweet talked her before resuming his work. The cat remained by his side.

Dad stood at the garage door. "That cat has hardly stirred away from this garage since the day you left," he said. Then noticing what Bob was doing, he added, "Taking the motor out for a little spin?"

"Something like that. Pop, will you follow me?"

"Sure. Where?"

"I'm going to Nick's service station on the hill," he said while fitting the tires in place, "I have some business to transact."

Dad had a quizzical expression.

Bob looked up. "Nick has always had an eye on this beauty and I know she would be in good hands with him."

"Are you thinking of selling your motorcycle?" Dad was astonished.

"No sense letting it sit here and collect dust," he said. "I don't know when I will get home again and when and if I do want to buy her back, I know Nick will sell it to me."

Dad shrugged and sighed. "Well, I guess you know what you're doing." Then he stood there in awe, wondering what else to say. "I'll go get the car keys."

Bewildered he told Mom what Bob was planning. She replied, "Any boy that can pass the requirements for pilot training in the United States Air Corps can certainly decide what to do with his own motorcycle."

Concern wrinkled his brow. "I hate to see him do it. He has loved tinkering with that thing. Why can't we keep it for him? I mean it seems so final."

Mom shook her head. "It's his decision, let him make it. Don't forget there will be other things to interest him when he gets out of the service. He is changing into manhood and parting with his last toy is proof that he is now a man! Don't you think?"

Bob climbed on the motorcycle, excited to hear the purr and feel the power run through the handle bars straight up his arms and into his body. He pressed his foot hard into the bottom of the black boot, and stood on the strong petal that cranked the motor. It missed. Standing up and placing all his weight on the one foot, he bounced on it again. It missed. He then turned the key in the ignition and pressed once again on the petal. The machine started with a roar. Bob laughed aloud. "A fine pilot I'm going to make. I can't even remember to turn on the ignition key!"

Affixing the clear riding goggles over his eyes, he accelerated the gas, kicked up the stand and roared down the driveway and out into the street. He waved to his father who sat in the Chevrolet ready to follow him.

The motorcycle was out of sight when his dad pulled out of the driveway, but he arrived at Nick's on the hill in time to see the sadness that covered his son's face as he transacted his business.

Bob forced a smile as he handed the ignition key and pink slip over to Nick. Taking one last check in the empty saddle bags, he patted the machine on the fender and looked upwards towards the sky. Another type of machine would replace the Harley Davidson just as it had replaced the Model A. He climbed in the front seat of the Chevy. "Well, that's that," he said. "Now I won't worry about it anymore. Come on, Pop, step on it. I have a date!"

"Pretty sweet on that girl, are you?" Dad asked.

Bob's solo plane.

Uncle Marshall taught Bob to fly.

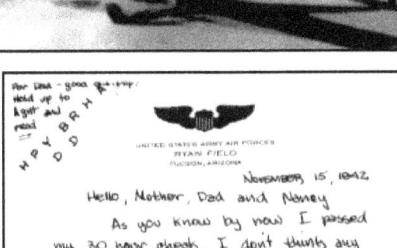

A letter from my brother - November 1942

A Trainer Plane
Flight Conference.

Receiving Trainer Plane
Flight Instructions.

Trainer Aircraft -
Ryan Field, Tucson, AZ.

Bob in a Trainer Plane.

"I guess so," Bob answered.

"What are your plans? I mean, are you going to do anything about it?"

"I can't plan anything yet for awhile," he said. "Uncle Sam has me tied up right now."

At home once again, Bob skipped up the front steps and bounded into the house. He spent the next hour soaking in a warm bathtub and singing – off key – at the top of his voice while Twinkletoes sat on the wash basin and contently purred with each encore.

Wrapped in a towel and gently shoving the cat out of the way he filled the washbasin with hot water and lathered his chin. After shaving he bent over to rinse off the foam when suddenly Twinkletoes jumped onto his back, peeked over his shoulder and purred in his ear.

"Be a good kitty and jump down," Bob pleaded, but the cat was content to stay where she was. So, he reached around, grabbed the cat by the neck and swung her high above onto the cornice box over the blinds and left her there meowing.

After he left we had a difficult time getting the cat down.

Bob's interest now was Dorothy Barbara. Borrowing the Chevy he drove to her house. She was waiting for him. They were both shy at first in front of her mother. They shook hands. "Ready?" he asked.

She nodded, said good-bye to her mother, grabbed her wrap and they walked hand in hand down the driveway to the little car where he immediately put his arm around her and drew her closer to him.

Dinner at our house was full of small talk by everyone but especially Dad who liked to tease about anything and now about the two young lovers. Bob told story after story of his days in training and everyone listened with interest, but it was obvious that the two lovers really wanted to be alone.

Too soon the 48 hour pass came to and end and it was time to say farewell again.

This time he would go to a new airfield in Tucson, Arizona.

V Don't Fence Me In

Headquarters
Santa Ana Army Air Base
Office of the commanding officer
Santa Ana, California
August 18, 1942
Dear Mrs. Remple,
It is with great pleasure that I notify you that your son, Robert C. Remple, has been selected by the Classification Board for Pilot training in the United States Army Air Forces. I congratulate both you and him on this achievement.

He will soon be transferred to one of the West Coast Army Air Forces Training Center elementary flying schools and will then begin his flight training. The course of instruction which he will pursue throughout the flying schools is thorough, intensive and the best that our Country can give to fit him for his future duties and responsibilities as a member of the Army Air Forces. Upon successful completion of his flying training, he will receive his Wings and the rating of air-plane Pilot.

In either war or peace, a Pilot occupies a position that requires sound judgment, a keen and alert mind, a sound body and the ability to perfectly coordinate mind and body in the flying of the airplane. It is imperative that the men who fly our military aircraft possess these qualifications, for upon their skill will depend in large measure the success of our war effort.

It is my hope that you will derive great satisfaction from your son's selection for Pilot training, and that his future career in the Army Air Forces will be one of continuing success and service.
Sincerely yours,
W.A. Robertson
Colonel, Army Air Forces,
Commanding

Music and songs kept people happy and humming in an attempt to forget the tragedies of war. Glenn Miller and his big band was the all time favorite. Most of the popular songs had to do with sweethearts missing each other while in the service and away from home. *"Give me one dozen roses, put my heart in beside them and send them to the one I love,"* was on the top of the charts.

Bob was now, Air Corps Cadet Robert C. Remple and proud of it.

The first week of Elementary Flying School was much like that at Santa Ana Army Air Corps Base, he wrote. Although Bob was now in Arizona, the weather varied little from the hot, dusty fields in California. There was a new routine to learn, new cadets to meet and a new cook with variations on how to prepare the food.

He was diligent in trying to answer all the letters from home; including those from relatives; Mother's sister, Frances Brown in particular and those of our neighbor Mary Kanagy, who had a slight friendly crush on Bob. They teased each other unmercifully and laughed a lot over the side fence separating the two properties. Mary was a Spanish dancer complete with castanets, a tight red dress with a ruffled skirt and heels clicking on the hardwood floors. Her mother played the piano while she practiced. Bob and Mary got along fine as neighbors and friends. They would tease each other continually but they did not hit it off romantically.

The Kanagy's had a beach house on a small man-made island called Balboa. It was located about 55 miles south of Los Angeles. Mr. Kanagy had purchased the land for the extravagant price of $200 and built a house around 1929. (Houses there today sell in the millions of dollars). Mr. Kanagy died shortly after that but Mrs. Kanagy held onto the property as a rental and summer home. Bob adored riding his motorcycle to Balboa Island, swimming in the Bay, clowning on the beach with a towel draped around him toga style, dancing at the Rendezvous Ballroom to the sounds of Big Bands, and just playing cards with his friends. Mrs. Kanagy was very generous with sharing the beach house with all of us. She loved having a houseful of young people for the weekend and Bob went every opportunity he had.

Mom wrote to Bob:
Los Angeles, California
Dear Son,
Twinkletoes is sitting here staring at me and meowing softly her 'hellos' to the only person she loves well enough to stand on his bare back while he shaves.

She is still trying to keep the Blue Jays from stealing all the walnuts off the tree but they are getting the best of her. She hunches her back and hisses at them but they dive down and peck her on the head. Then she runs as fast as she can under the porch.

Whenever I come home she is always waiting for me with a yawn. She stretches her paws and rubs against my legs. Your cat is either pestering the birds or me.

It was really nice we got to see you this weekend. Be sure to send your new address when you are transferred.

Love from your mother and of course, Twinkletoes.

A letter from Ryan Field, Arizona showed a design on the stationary of a silhouetted cactus on the desert with a plane flying over.

Ryan Field, Tucson Arizona   August 25, 1942
Dear Mother and Dad,

Well, here I am. It is so hot here that we do not wear neckties and that is something for the Army!!! The 'field' is 20 miles from hotter Tucson. This is a brand new place. We are the third class of 200 to be here. No telephones, no telegraph and only old plumbing connected. All I can see is desert with mountains in the distance.

We just had a dilly of a storm and all the hot weather turned cold. Planes danced about and it was really something. Aside from that, school and flying are advancing fine. I am glad I have had some flying experience. It has not helped much because the planes are so different, but I have confidence and am more relaxed than I would be without any.

Bob was just finishing the letter when suddenly the door blew open and with it came a husky O.D. blowing a whistle and shouting, "Everybody outside. The wind is making scrap metal of those planes out there. We've got to tie them down."

Tommy, a slim six-foot two Texan collided with Bob as they ran out the door. Tommy was a real Texan and proud of it. The only thing he liked near as much as Texas was flying. He and Bob had that in common and would remain friends throughout their training.

It was a couple of weeks before he finished the letter.

October 6, 1942
Mother, Dad & Nancy

I really am sorry I didn't write sooner, but maybe you know by now that there isn't much time.

If I had to ride on a train more than one day I would become a conscientious objector. Maybe that two in a "lower" had something to do with it. They were good Pullmans and dinners but it sure is dirty traveling – at least I think so.

This field is almost new. I am in the third class here. There is inspection only once a week on Saturdays. Open post – no passes required – on Wednesday night 5:00 – 10:00 and weekends, Saturday noon to Sunday at 6:00. All this time with nothing to do. There isn't a good restaurant in the whole town – what a place –

So far it has rained twice – last night and this afternoon. There was more <u>wind</u>!, lightning and thunder than rain.

We were called out to hold down the planes but before we got there three of them were blown loose and one damaged beyond repair, the other two will be repaired. Lightning struck one plane and jumped from one to another. We have hangers but they are used for overhauling planes. The other planes are lined up on the "flight line" in long lines – real long there are 100 planes. I guess it's not restricted – I hope. Things sure come fast – in school and in flying. I'm glad I've had some flying – it doesn't help much, but I'm more confident and relaxed than I would be without it. These planes are altogether different then anything I've been in. They land faster than any other primary or even a basic trainer. They hit the ground from 90 to 80 mph and that's fast! The old cub that I soloed landed at 30 mph. So to learn over again – I hope.

The ride on the train was impressive, you should have seen the freight coming the other way.

Well, I didn't intend to write another page. I don't know what to say.

How do you like your job now – Dad? I think of you and home often, but I'm not lonely or homesick so don't think about it. But on Sundays I miss seeing good old L.A... If anyone sayzzz anything about California – well they had better not be from Arizona – hot desolate country.
Good bye for now – Love, Bob

Hardships and shortages became a way of life on the home front. If anyone complained, they got a strong retort, "Don't you know there's a war on?" The war changed everything. Those who suffered from unemployment or left over from the depression soon found jobs. The opening of Military Bases and Defense Plants employed millions, but still left some without jobs.

Even school was changed by the war. A Defense Saving Bonds

program went into each classroom of every school. Students brought their dimes or quarters each week to purchase a stamp. The stamp went into a savings book. When the book was filled, you turned it into the bank and they issued a $25 Savings Bond in your name. Sometimes Mother only had twenty-five cents to spare. Other times she would give me a whole dollar and I could buy 4 stamps at a time. At a dime a stamp, the ten cent books took longer to fill.

Everyone was required to bring a pillow from home to be left at school for the bomb drills. These occurred whenever Miss Fitzroy, the Principal, so desired. Miss Fitzroy had a man's hair cut, wore tailored suits and blouses and meant business. She never smiled. She tried to catch us off guard by setting the alarm off when we least expected it. Classrooms emptied out as quickly as possible into the smelly hallways. There we sat on the cold cement, back to the wall, waiting for the all-clear. I couldn't figure out the logic of the drills. If we were to be bombed, what difference would it make if we were in the classroom or the hall? The whole building would get it! And it seemed quite remote to me that the "Japs" would single out 59th Street Elementary School to destroy.

Echoing through the halls were the upraised voices of hundreds of children singing, *God Bless America* and *The Star Spangled Banner*. A teacher would blow a pitch pipe and hum, "Hmmmm," and we would hum back. Then we sang, *Don't Fence Me In* and *Deep in the Heart of Texas* – clap! clap! clap! until we were thoroughly tired of the songs. Just when our tail bones were about to crack, the all-clear sounded and we could go back to our classrooms.

Every class had a garden patch to maintain. The boys worked the "Victory Gardens" and supplied the cafeteria with lettuce, carrots, celery, squash, beets and any vegetable that would grow in adobe soil. The girls knitted afghan squares from scratchy wool yarn. Later the many squares were sewn together to make a lap robe. What puzzled me was what happened to all the afghans that were made? Where did they go? Every school made them. Newsreels never showed any GI soldier, sailor or marine wrapped in an afghan that we had made.

Being liberated women, even in third grade, we claimed our rights to work in the garden. So one day our teacher switched jobs. The girls got to hoe and irrigate the vegetables while the boys learned to knit. We loved it and from that time on we took turns. Boys in the garden one day, girls the next.

In the summer time, and whenever she could horde enough sugar, Mother would can fruit and jam. Even though we still had jars of peaches left from the year before, she would can more. Neighbors with over-bearing trees supplied the fruit, Mother supplied the labor and we all benefited by it in the winter months when fresh fruit was scarce.

Ryan Field,
Tucson, Arizona

> October 18, 1942
> Dear Mother, Dad and Nancy,
>
> It has just rained again. Everything is going swell. If all goes well, and it will, it will only be six more weeks here and then basic. I hope it will be closer.
>
> I got a letter from (uncle) Marshall. It was sent to SAAB Have you heard anything about him? There's not much to write about – all I can think of is flying and Dorothy.
>
> Last Sunday seems like it was years ago. I don't think it'll come in on weekends any more.
>
> The 1000 navy men moved in! They are all newly commissioned ensigns and Lt. J.G.'s. My arm is worn out (saluting them). I wonder how they feel?
>
> I finally got my last shot Saturday!
>
> Dad, how is your new job? I suppose there is as much loafing there as at Northrup.
>
> This is all – just a few lines to keep up the good work. Thanx.
>
> Love, Bob
>
> P.S. Nancy,
> How is school? Are you using my notebook? Tell Mary (the girl next door) hello for me. Be a good girl. Goodbye, Bob
>
> P.S. Find out from Dorothy what she wants of my drafting things. (Her brother needed to borrow his drafting instruments for a class).

Dorothy Barbara suggested they go to Arizona some weekend and offered to pay for part of the gas. Mother thought it was a great idea and got the ball rolling in that direction. Dad was not hard to convince. It was a long hot drive, but the reward at the end was worth it.

Bob was looking forward to his folks and Dorothy Barbara coming for the weekend.

Unlike the greeting they gave him at SAAAB, Mother was now shocked at his appearance. His skin was pale and cheeks hollow, dark circles formed pools under his eyes. His exhausted appearance prompted immediate concern from the ones that loved him. But he laughed at her concern. "Don't you know I'm big enough to wipe my own nose? There's nothing wrong with me, it's just you haven't seen me for some time. As a matter of fact, you look great – all of you!" And he embraced all three of them.

"So, what shall we do? What would you like to see? I've got a 24 hour pass. We can do anything you want to do in one day."

Dad wanted to see the planes Bob was flying. A school of students were just boarding their planes the same way Bob had been doing for five weeks. The light planes taxied to the runway and lifted off the ground like they were a feather scooped into the sky by a light updraft of wind and left floating there.

Mother wished he would be home for Thanksgiving but his answer was, "I doubt it. We'll probably carry on the same routine here with perhaps a little turkey dinner thrown in on the side. When the enemy takes time off for holidays, then I guess the army will."

So thrilled to see Dorothy Barbara again, he could hardly talk. After dinner they had planned to see a movie, but Mother and Dad, wanting to give them some time together, retired early to the Motel and let Bob use the car. Neither one of them wanted to spend their precious time together watching a movie. They preferred to be together to talk and make plans for the future. The night turned into day without either one sleeping so when Bob returned to the base, his eyes burned but his heart felt light.

The warmth of Dorothy Barbara in his arms was still with him. He yawned and hoped he would not have to fly today, having stayed up all night with his new girlfriend. However there was little doubt in his mind that he would not have to fly; having 30 hours to catch up on meant everyday flying for a week.

The barracks was empty when Bob returned. He rushed into his wool flying suit, pulled up the zippers on the sleeves, then bending over to zip up the bottom of the legs, he felt like a well-stuffed Santa Claus. With one last tug, he pulled the zipper up the front. The suit was warm in the room but upstairs in the heavens the warmth would feel good and sometimes it still was not enough to shut out the unearthly cold. He left the barracks and headed for the field. Hailing a passing jeep, he hitched a ride the rest of the way. At the field an instructor said he had an extra hour and would go up with Bob to make the corrections he had been worried about.

They climbed into the cockpit of the PT-24. The instructor

sitting in the front and Bob at the controls behind him. The clearance signal was given and Bob took the plane up in a perfect take off. He hoped the rest of the flight went as well. After a short cruise away from the field the instructor said, "I'll show you. First start with a slow roll. Roll her over slowly on her back. Now bring back the controls on the path."

The ship rolled over the rest of the way and righted itself.

"All right," said the instructor. "Now you do it."

Bob rolled the ship up-side-down and there they hung by their safety belts. The instructor said nothing. Bob tried to reach the rudder pedal but his feet insisted on hanging down and he could not hold onto his thoughts. But remembering what his dad had said, "You can do it if you really put your mind to it," and after what seemed to be an endless amount of time, Bob righted the ship.

"Okay," said the instructor, "now a snap roll. Same thing only quicker."

Without further difficulties and ready to tackle anything, Bob pulled through the rest of the acrobatic exercises. He was beginning to feel frisky, daring and serenely confident when he looked out the side cockpit window. There were other planes going through the same maneuvers. He smiled with confidence until he saw a plane lose control. It started to spin and plummeted towards the ground.

"Pull up," he said to himself. But the plane spun like a toy top and smashed into the hard earth. Nobody jumped out and the little plane burst into flame.

Bob landed the PT-24 in silence, taking the warning in good measure. Once on the ground the instructor referred to the accident. "We've had plenty of boys get overconfident and that's where they end up. Last week one fellow came in for a landing, bounced up in the air, got excited and shoved the stick forward and opened the throttle. The plane nosed into the ground and plowed up quite a bit of runway." He paused and added. "Come out tomorrow. I'll give you a final check."

    Ryan Field
    Tucson, Arizona
    October 22, 1942
    Dear Mother and Dad, Nancy and kitty,

Dorothy said that you haven't received a letter. You should have, I wrote one the first of the week, after the weekend you were here. I sent it before I received your first letter.

I went to church last night. I think it will help. There are times I sure need it. I also met – last Sunday – the camp welfare worker. He comes to camp once a week on Wednesdays. There was a girl there that contacts all the boys who are interested in church and arranges parties for them with girls from the University of Arizona. I don't think I'm interested very much but it's something to do sometime, maybe.

I should solo today. I go up in an hour or so. I'll tell you before I finish this letter. Over 25% of our fellows have been eliminated so far – when it's going to stop, I don't know. There are some things that I MUST correct if I expect to go on, but I know that everything will be alright.

It sure is getting cold in the mornings! I wonder how much it would cost to send that LONG underwear? And P.J.'s. I'm going to write Mary (next door neighbor) *soon, but tell her that the sweater comes in mighty handy in the morning.*

Some of the fellows that are graduating get a few days furlough. They (some of them) are arranging to get rides home in planes (B-24's) from that field near Tucson, maybe when my time comes (if and when) I'll be able to do the same – to be cont'd after flying solo – I hope!

"I Doded It!"

I went over to one of our auxiliary fields. I made three landings with the instructor. Each time I landed we would taxi back around to the take off strip. The third time he told me to stop the ship, that he had had enough and for me to take it around, so I did. I made three landings, all of them were - well not bad, and not good – but I did it any way.

The job is far from done, I got to keep 'on the ball.' There are constant reminders – fellows are still dropping by the wayside. The upper class is just about through and some of them don't pass their check rides!

There are 4 check rides given, a 10 hour check, 30 hr, 50hr and a final 60 hour. These are not given exactly on time. I'll have my 10 hour check soon.

Dorothy said that I should be ashamed of myself for not writing oftener but - - I'm sorry. I think she feels, well I don't know what, but she gets all the letters and you get none, don't blame her, she wants me to write to you as much as you do. I'll write more. Good Bye, Love, Bob

P.S. How's your job, Pop? Hello Nancy, how's my sister? (He always remembered me!}

Dad sat at the kitchen table pouring warmed over yesterday's coffee into a cup. He stirred the muddy black liquid and sipped it. "There's a rumor circulating that some of us over 50 are going to be laid off," he told Mother. "I finally get a few weeks work, then it blows up in my face!"

Mother told him not to worry that he'd find another job. "You always have."

"That's the trouble," he said, "I've had job after job but nothing steady. I tell you, men like me just aren't needed in this changing world. A man my age has got to have an education or be a farmer."

Mother tried to console him. "You are a superb salesman. It's not your fault there is a war and jobs are scarce. You'll find something."

Dad shook his head. "Bob must have a pretty low opinion of his father."

> Ryan Field
> Tucson, Arizona
> October 25, 1942
> Dear Mother & Dad
> Say – Dad are you on some special investigating committee that is checking up on war production in all those plants? The job as crane operator takes a lot of experience before you get real good. I hope you will like it.
> Where is (uncle) Marshall now and what kind of a ship is he flying?
> If George Hay needs any encouragement to come – well give it to him. I probably won't see him again for the duration.
> I really don't know what to say. It was good to talk to you on the phone this morning. What about those pictures that (uncle) Harold took? Say hello to him for me.
> I am planning on going to church every Wednesday night. I'll be thinking of you going to church as I am leaving. I don't have much time to read the (Bible) lesson- just enough for one section and I read over one or two of the songs in that book you gave me. It's easier to remember phrases that rhyme.
> Well I guess that's all until I get your letter with questions I can answer – but don't ask too many. Love, Bob

Harold was a second cousin of Mother's and had a hobby of taking pictures. Badly bent over with rheumatism and arthritis and hard of hearing, he took forever to set up his tripod, take a light reading, adjust the lens and before he could snap the picture the subject – often my cousin and I - would be through smiling and posing and ready to move on. He was thrilled when someone appreciated his efforts as a photographer.

>Ryan Field
>Tucson, Arizona
>*October 31, 1942 (morning)*
>*Dear Folks and Nancy*
>*Thanks for the letters. And thanks for the long underwear and pajamas. They got here just in time. Brrr. I'm shivering right now – and it's after 10am. About 1 or 2 o'clock it will be hot enough to run around in gym shorts. The cookies are all gone. They are sure good, but all the food we get here is starch. All the vegetables we get are from cans. A lot of the fellows have rashes on their skin. Everybody says it's the diet. Could be...? We have a menu posted, they sound good. "Fresh garden peas" – (from cans)*
>*"Salted wafers" (crackers)*
>*"Fresh creamed Dairy butter" (same old butter I've always used)*
>*"Raisin bread" (never saw any)*
>*"Ice cream and wafers" (good ice cream but where were the wafers?)*
>*So I enjoy the cookies but it's more starch. I don't know what to say about more.*
>*I passed my 10 hour check yesterday. The upper-classmen left for basic – at Bakersfield! – last night. Now we are upper-classmen. That means that I will be here only for 4 more weeks. (I'm so cold I can't think as well as write). We're waiting for inspection and all the windows must be open – and this cement floor is <u>cold</u>!*
>*I am going to save my money (what money?) for the future - it not only would be nice, but it is a necessity.*
>*I must say good by for now – if I want to get this off before Monday.*
>*Love, Bob*

(At the bottom of his letter was a drawing of a face with only a nose and fingers peeking over a fence or a straight line. Underneath was written KILROY WAS HERE.

(There really was a Kilroy. His name was James J. Kilroy. During WWII he worked at the Ford River Shipyard as a "checker", noting the number or rivets driven by workers who did piecework and were paid by the rivet. Kilroy would put a check mark in chalk after the block counted so it would not be counted twice. But some riveters would erase the mark after Kilroy was off duty so they would get paid when another checker came by. When the boss asked why these riveters were getting so much pay, Kilroy said he would look into it. So he started writing in big letters with crayon – KILROY WAS HERE. Ordinarily any marks would be painted over before a ship shipped out. But there was a war on and the ships were leaving the shipyard so fast, there wasn't time to paint them. Kilroy's inspection "trademark" was seen by thousands of servicemen using those ships. And so the slogan caught on).

President Franklin D. Roosevelt made speeches all the time and broadcast on the radio: "There had never been – there never can be – a successful compromise between good and evil. Only total victory can reward the champions of tolerance and decency and freedom and faith," he said. I was very proud of my brother serving his country and I bragged to everyone about him being in the Air Force.

VI Rosie the Riveter

Ryan Field
Tucson, Arizona

November 3, 1942

Dear Mother and Dad – and Nancy,

If you and Dorathy exchange letters there's not much to write about that you haven't already heard, although I know you would rather have me tell you than hear it from Dorathy Barbara, I mean first hand.

I am (the whole post) restricted to the post for an indefinite time. The new class was supposed to be exposed to scarlet fever – how about that? Some fun! Find out if S.A.A.A.B is quarantined. I can't see that it's practical, the civilians come and go all day and they are exposed to the underclass as much or more than we are, but that's the army. We also had to move into some nice new barracks, dusty, no water, six bare light bulbs and no heat.

The ride on the B-24 was sure educational. I would have written to you last night about it but I started a letter to D. B. when I had to move and just had time to finish it. I rode in every conceivable place in the bomber (except the pilot's seat). They used that Norton bomb sight for practice bombing. All the bombardier has to do is set a lot of gauges, dials, etc, tell the pilot to turn a little to the left – a little to the right, steady – then back and forth some more, more gauge setting then more moving back and forth – then zip goes the bomb! I don't want to fly one of these – there like trucks, big cumbersome things, but I wouldn't want to attack one of them – machine guns are all over the thing. (Author's note: In 1998, I climbed inside a B-17 and a B-24 and could not believe how small and how cramped it was! There was very little room to move around. And the pilot's area was especially tight. At the time I thought how small the young men had to be to fit in the plane. I guess it was considered big in 1942).

My flying is just so – so. I can't seem to decide if it's fair – or no good! I am flying an hour solo and an hour dual – that's not fun *any more, its <u>work</u> and I am tired!! It's both mental and physical so as Mary would probably say, "I won't last much longer."*

I'll write you a better letter again. Good night. (Drawing of a guy on a cot zzzzz snoring).

Love, Bob

Mother made an announcement that startled everyone in the family. She was going to start working in a defense plant on the assembly line. This was a little shocking as she had not worked since she was a nurse before getting married. And now she would be wearing coveralls instead of a white uniform. Around her head she tied a red bandana scarf instead of the jaunty white starched nurse's hat. And the boots! That was really out of character but she took it all in her stride, carried her lunch in a pail and climbed in the back of a truck with other women heading for Lockheed Defense Plant. It wasn't long before women all over the country were signing up to do men's work in the factories building ships and planes. Ads were placed in magazines to get women's attention encouraging them to "hasten victory by working and saving your man." And, "The more women at work, the sooner we win." This was to help the war effort and allow the eligible men to join the armed forces. These women soon got the title of "Rosie the Riveter". (Rosie the Riveter got her start when a song was written by Redd Evans and John Loeb in 1942 with a catchy tune and lyrics. Everyone was singing, "Rosie, the riveter." Then one day the Hollywood star, Walter Pigeon was touring the Ford Motor Company aircraft assembly plant and met a woman named Rose Monroe and he recommended she play a part in a promotional film about the war effort, so the story goes. The famous illustrator Norman Rockwell picked up on the popularity of the fictional character and created a "Rosie" for the cover of the Saturday Evening Post magazine showing a woman wearing a scarf around her head, goggles and flexing her biceps with a rolled-up sleeve. Printed in bold letters were WE CAN DO IT! The image became a huge success and "Rosie" became an icon. More stories appeared in the press of other "Rosies". Songs, plays and movies were made about "Rosie the Riveter." Women increased the work force by fifty percent).

Mom was concerned that her job might be an embarrassment to her son. But D.B. assured her he would be proud of his patriotic mother.

Bob commented on his mother's ambition in one of his letters, *"What do you know about that? I never would have guessed my very own mother would be making airplanes for me to fly! I'm sure they will never fall apart now."*

Mother assured Bob that she checked and double checked her work and then a foreman came along and checked again. *"The entire division is comprised of mothers whose sons are serving the country,"* she wrote to him. *"Don't worry, we won't let you down."* Dad added a note. *"And you ought to see her muscles. They're bigger than mine! What is the world coming to? First women take over wearing trousers, and then they're sprouting muscles big enough to give a blacksmith competition."*

Dad too was working in a defense plant as a guard at Douglas Aircraft Company, having left the crane operator job that he held for a short time. My parents would work split shifts so someone would be around to take care of me. And Dad ashamed that he could not get work elsewhere pleaded with Mother to not let Bob know he was only a guard in a defense plant.

> Ryan Field
> Tucson, Arizona
> *November 6, 1942*
> *Dear Mother, Dad and Nancy*
> *Another week gone by and I am still here. Three more left after Wednesday.*
> *Yesterday I had my parachute on from 12:45 to 6:45. During that time I was either flying or being refueled and checking out with the dispatcher. I was in the air for three hours. After the first half hour it ceases to be fun. I didn't fly straight or level once. It is always spins, stalls, lazy (you feel lazy after doing them for 3 hours) eights, chandelles, and S's across the road. I have over 25 hours now; my 30 hour check (not check up) sometime next week. The ones that pass this are almost sure of getting thru primary.*
> *We have a new C.O. he is a first lieutenant and this is his first time as C.O. I wish they would quit experimenting on us. As you know we have closed post. To make it enjoyable our C.O. has seen to it that we won't have to strain ourselves mentally trying to think of something to do. We have athletics from 1 p.m. to 5 p.m. and Sunday from 8 a.m. to 3 p.m., then a Chaplin is coming and it is compulsory for every one to attend. In the evenings we <u>may</u> study if we care to or write letters that we <u>might</u> care to write.*
> *Right now the boys are playing baseball and I am sitting in an empty barracks (unused) writing. There are a few things on my*

mind (and I imagine so do some of these other fellows) I would like to tell him, but – he is an "officer". He is working out for the upper class. (Not sure here if he is referring to the C.O., who apparently was not very well liked and they wanted to tell him where to go. Or was he referring to the Chaplain and wanting to tell him what was in his heart). *We play baseball and talk with the lower class men (who were exposed to scarlet fever) but they cannot mingle with us in the P.X. or recreation hall. If you can make sense of this, let me know.*

While on inspection (by the way, our barracks was the only one to pass inspection) a few of the boys didn't keep eyes front. Our dear C.O. had them stand at attention facing each other. He said that well disciplined soldiers could look at each other without laughing. So after looking at each other they both started to laugh. Now they are walking tours – to make them disciplined. Now I have learned the smaller the officer, the bigger he thinks he is.

Day before yesterday I had my 90 degree accuracy landings. That is, to approach the runway at 90 degrees and cut the throttle (let up on the gas) and glide into the field making a 90 degree turn. Then the landings were supposed to alternate, one beyound a white line across the field and the next one in front of the line. Seven planes take part at one time. We have a pattern to follow around the field. When we are spaced evenly there is just enough room to land as the one in front takes off. (See diagram). This takes about 45 minutes. When I was <u>through</u>, I was through. I don't know of more of strain than flying like this, or during any test. If the fellow in front of me makes his pattern to far away from the field the rest would have to follow in order to keep from catching up with him. Then I would have to climb higher or leave power on until I got up to my turn into the field, so that I could glide into the field without dropping short of the runway. In that case the gas would be opened to make the field. Every time that happened it would discount from our grade (the individual's grade). The fellow in front of me had to use power 3 times when he should have been gliding. He failed, but he has two more chances. There is still another 150 degree accuracy landing test to go. That will be next week also. I don't think it will be much different.

We were issued new flying suits a few days ago. They are like the zute suits, but they are wool. They have zippers along the sleeves and around the bottoms of the legs and another one up the front. Now it isn't so cold upstairs.

The boys are demolishing about two planes per week. To see the planes you wonder how the fellows got out with out a scratch, but they do.

I had my picture taken for our Wind-Sock, with our class – something like an annual book. Helmet and goggles were standard equipment (with horns). I could have some made, but with those horns and the over eager expression upon my face (?) is too much.

I was going to write yesterday but it would have been useless to ask you, Pop, how you like your "new" job with Associated Pipe and Steel? You ought to go on Hobby Lobby. Sooner or later you will find a job you are suited for, so I guess it is not so bad to look for one.

Our instructors only work half a day or when our group flies. This way the instructors work to Friday noon and don't have to be back until Monday noon. Mine took a day off and went to L.A. I sure wish that I could have gone with him, but he had a car load. So-o-o, I'll try again. I can't leave Thanksgiving and I have my doubts about any other time. Our class is behind schedule, that's why I have to fly from 2 to 3 hours a day, and we can't spare a moment.

(Author's note: It's incredible how hard these young men trained to fly planes for the war effort without a thought of what lie before them).

When I get a letter with a lot of questions I forget them, and if I look them up, reading the letter over it doesn't leave much time to write. I haven't much time, because I am having to study more in less time. If I don't get time to write to Frances (aunt) *tell her that any thing homemade with or without black walnuts will be accepted with open arms.*

I must say good-bye now, I am thinking of you...
Love, Bob

Black-outs went into affect soon after the bombing of Pearl Harbor. Windows were draped with black cloth or black-out curtains to keep any light from showing on the outside, just in case the enemy might be flying over, or a Japanese spy might be walking down the street.

Air Raid drills were held once a week in our neighborhood. When the siren roared, every house went dark and people stayed inside. I didn't like these drills and felt relieved when the 'all-clear' sounded. Dad volunteered to be a block Air Raid Warden to enforce the black out regulations.

We had black shades on the windows and even though the

lights were turned off, the shades had to be pulled down past the sill. It was impressed upon me the importance of keeping those shades closed.

One night was especially scary. The sirens blared. It was later than usual when the alarm sounded. I was already in bed and asleep when the noise shattered the stillness, awakening me. My heart began to pound. Mother had gone off to the graveyard shift at the factory and Dad being the block captain had to go out and check the houses for any lights showing. He was getting ready to do just that. I watched him pick up his white helmet with the volunteer logo sticker on it and his civil defense arm band and place them on the various parts of his anatomy. Then he picked up the flash light and fire extinguisher that he kept ready by the front door, told me to leave the shades down and go back to bed and he'd be back as soon as he could.

"Lights out!" he called to the neighbors.

I was eight years old, alone and scared. The alarm kept going. Something was going on. I peeked under the shade out the window. The sky was lit up with wild beams of blue lights making patterns over the palm trees. I stuck my head under the forbidden shade. I wished the sirens would stop screaming. The blackness was interrupted by a circle of search lights surrounding an object that moved across the sky. In the network of lights was an airplane and then much to my astonishment, short flashes of fire began shooting up from the ground towards the plane. My heart beat was now choking me. The sirens continued to scream. What was going on? The plane was being fired upon. I was held in a trance of wonderment. Were we under attack like Pearl Harbor? Were there real bullets flashing in the sky or was I dreaming? The blue lights followed the plane for what seemed to be an hour but was probably only a few minutes. The plane was moving toward the Pacific Ocean. The anti-aircraft followed it and continued firing like it was trying to scare it away.

The plane was soon out of sight but the bluish lights still created a criss-cross pattern in the night sky. I was glad when the all-clear alarm sounded and happier still when Dad returned home. I asked him if it was a real Japanese plane, but he thought it was only a practice drill.

(This incident was on February 24, 1942. Sometime later a report came out in Life Magazine that a Japanese plane was spotted over Los Angeles and was downed at Hermosa Beach. Others have said there was no plane sighted. However I saw a plane flying above the palm trees and caught in the search lights). And only a few days before that incident, a Japanese submarine was spotted off the coast of Goleta, California. The war was closer than I wanted it to be).

Soon after this incident I went skipping into Jergins' Market by myself and didn't notice anything unusual. The floor was swept clean, the rows of oranges were placed in perfect pyramids with care. Each apple was polished to a high gloss. But Mr. Kajima was not there. Mr. Jergins saved sweets behind the counter for his customers. When I came in he winked and motioned me over. "Look what I have today." He pulled out a tray of candy and put it on the glass counter.

I pointed to the marshmallow look-a-like-ice cream cones and the tootsie rolls. "Those look good. I need some for Janie too."

Mr. Jergin's merry face drooped. His red-hair toupee was on crooked this day, the part was far off center and the whole piece was too much over his forehead to look right. I thought it would fall off when he leaned down for the candy. But that was not why he was frowning. Something was wrong. It seemed that every day the war news got worse and I didn't want any more bad news, so I thanked him and ran past the produce counters and into the backroom, through the flimsy curtain door calling out, "Janie! Janie! It's me! Look what I brought!" There was no answer. The room was empty. There were no familiar tea cups or Japanese newspapers on the table. The mats were rolled up on the cots. Janie's orange crate desk was empty. Her crayolas were gone. The musty smell of damp gunny sacks, old onions and rotting fruit filled my nose. The sawdust had been swept up into a corner and the packing crates were stacked to one side. There was not a trace or shred of evidence that anyone had every lived in the backroom. Where did they go in such a hurry? I stood there a few moments; the candy squished in my hands, then spun around and ran out, crying, "Mr. Jergins, Janie is gone!"

He looked sad. "They had to go away," he said almost apologetically.

"Why? Where did they go? Janie didn't tell me she was leaving." I had played ball in the alley with her only two days before.

"She didn't know she was," he replied.

"Where did they go?" I asked.

A large tear rolled down his chubby cheek.

"Are they coming back?"

Mr. Jergins took out a handkerchief from his apron pocket and blew his nose. "They went away in a truck. They've gone to a detention camp. It's the war!" he said shaking his head. "It's the war!"

Absently I started out of the store. I felt lost. On the side of the building was an ugly sign. "Instructions to all persons of JAPANESE ancestry ....will be evacuated...."I couldn't read all the words. What was happening to our nice neighborhood?

"Tell your mother to bring in her sugar coupons. I have sugar today," he called after me as I left.

I nodded and slowly walked home, wondering what was going on. Why were the Japanese families being imprisoned? They hadn't done anything. The war was far away across the ocean. Pearl Harbor had been bombed by the Japanese Military but that had nothing to do with Janie?

When I got home Mother was ready to leave for work. She was wearing her blue denim coveralls over her stubby body and a red bandana to cover her short-bobbed hair to keep flying particles from lodging in her hair. She looked as happy as a child about to go to a party. I think she enjoyed her job. It was the patriotic thing to do – working for the war effort.

She picked up her lunch pail and headed for the back door. "There's meatloaf in the refrigerator for dinner. Just stick it in the oven at 350 degrees with the potatoes for baking – on the sink. You'll be all right until your dad comes home?" It was a question and statement at the same time.

"Janie's gone," I was able to squeeze out.

Outside a horn honked. It was her ride. She opened the door and looked out. A truck, resembling a modern Conestoga wagon, waited by the curb. She tried to comfort me. "I can't take time to explain now," she said. "But Janie's Japanese."

"I know that," I said. "She was teaching me to read Japanese."

"Well, we're at war with Japan," she said.

I knew that too.

"They had to take all the Japanese away to camps." She paused briefly. "Because of spies," she said hurriedly.

"Janie's not a spy! She didn't start the war. Neither did her little sister or mother or father! They only sell carrots and potatoes!"

The horn honked again. Clucking sounds of women's voices fell out of the back end of the truck.

"I know, I know" she said. "Look, I have to run. Janie will be all right. We'll talk later."

I watched her climb under the flowered curtain which hung down the back of the truck. Inside four ladies were already there - waiting. They drove away. I was alone in an empty house. I felt alone in the world. Bob and his buddies were gone. Now Janie was gone. What next?

Mother wrote to Bob:

Twinkletoes is still missing you. When I come home from work in the mornings she yawns, stretches her legs, spreads her paws and rubs against my legs. I don't think she likes the idea of me wearing slacks any more than your father likes them.

This grave yard shift I'm working sounds much like the schedule you're keeping. After breakfast, I shower and crawl in bed under my eye-shade and attempt to sleep. Your cat likes to jump on the bed and look at me. If the phone rings I ignore it. The front door bell rings, I ignore it. With all this noise I get only a little sleep but I am home days and forced to keep my home clean in spite of my job. The weekends are what throw me really off schedule. Like tonight – Sunday. I have to sleep tonight and be up all night tomorrow. Oh, well, I suppose I'll adjust sooner or later. Some of the gals work seven days a week. That's not for me.

Everyone here sends their love.

Love, Mom and Pop

Sleeping during the day was difficult for Mom. She slept with a black eyeshade that covered half her face. I thought she looked like the Lone Ranger. Even with the eye shade she had trouble sleeping during the day. There was too much going on and too much to do. And she couldn't wait for the mail to arrive. Hopefully there was a letter from Bob which she would read to me.

VII I'll Be Seeing You

Ryan Field
November 10, 1942
Hello! Mother, Dad and Nancy,
   I am still in quarantine, but I think it will be lifted by this weekend. There isn't a trace of any fever here.
   Now I have 31 hours, that's four hours behind schedule. It means flying an hour extra for a week or a total of three hours. My 30 hour check will probably be this week. In the last five days I have had only three hours of time with my instructor, so I can't really tell if I am doing my maneuvers correct. I think I am doing something right, but my instructor will show me my mistake and I know, but lately he hasn't had time to go up with me. Everything is happening so fast, only twelve flying days with 30 hours to get in. If a strong wind or rain comes it means more hours in the day. If I'm not gray when I get out of training I'll be surprised.
   I'm almost through with my class in aircraft engines with meteorology to follow.
   After having $10 deducted from my pay for our dances (two of them) recreation supplies (ping pong balls etc. that are never seen) and pictures for the "Wind Sock" our dear Commandant of Cadets (not the C.O. as I have said) informed us that we could not publish our graduation magazine. All this was to use up the $10, for 200 cadets - that makes $2000. Where does it all go?
   It's getting time for bed and I have been ready to go to bed since dinner. I hear it is dark in L.A. at night, I sure would like to be back for a few days. One of the boys broke his finger. He can't fly until it heals. He is getting a furlough and a bomber ride home to North Carolina. Should I? (Drawing of upside down plane, pilot hanging upside down saying, hello Nancy). More later....
   The underclass are sure wrecking the planes. Last week one fellow came in for a landing, bounced up in the air and I guess he got excited – he shoved the stick forward and opened the throttle.

The airplane nosed down into the ground and plowed up quite a bit of the runway.

I had Thanksgiving off. (This letter dated Nov. 10th said he had Thanksgiving off. The letter dated Nov. 22nd said he wasn't going to get home for Thanksgiving. Perhaps he lost track of the dates. It wouldn't be hard with how active he was kept). *It was a surprise. I went into town and had a very good dinner – for a change. The food we get here, what there is of it, has caused most of the fellows, including me, to get kind of a rash on our skin – but not for long. On to Basic!*

I can think of flying those B.T's (basic trainers) now that I have passed all my checks. When I started here it seemed like something that you hear about and never reach that stage. Now my goal is advanced. That is nine weeks away. So far I have passed through part where most of the fellows have been eliminated. The average at basic is 3% to 5%. In advanced it is 1% so – it looks pretty good.

At basic (now that I can afford to talk about it) I will have instrument – or "blind" flying, night flying, cross country trips, formation flying and a little aerobatics.

I'll let you know as soon as possible where I am going and what my address is...

Love, Bob

Dad was changing jobs frequently. Having left the guard position at Douglas Aircraft Company, he was then employed for a short time at Associated Pipe and Steel, but that wouldn't last either. His main concern was his son. How he hoped and prayed that his son would do better with his life than his dad had done.

Savage jungle fighting was going on at Guadalcanal. The marines and army forced the Japanese to retreat. The naval battle was not going well in the Pacific. Carriers were sunk and Admiral Halsey asked for help. I hated hearing the news. It was scary. It sounded as if the war was getting worse instead of better. "When will it be over?" I asked. No one seemed to know.

War posters with slogans cleverly advertised were slapped on bill boards all over town. They were aimed at shaping American opinion, to get the young to enlist in the armed services, or to get volunteers for something, or to just encourage patriotism and help the war effort. Fear, anger, hatred, duty, sacrifice, guilt, patriotism, destroy the foe, were the themes.

UNCLE SAM WANTS YOU!

LOOSE LIPS SINK SHIPS REMEMBER December 7th 1941 – Pearl Harbor

DEFEND YOUR COUNTRY – ENLIST NOW

THE WALLS MAY HAVE EARS

Some advocated hating persons and nationalities rather than hatred of evil. They used words like AXIS and HITLER and the ENEMY. Some were too scary to look at. But the best looking one was of ROSIE THE RIVETER with her pretty face yet flexing her arm muscle and looking ready to work.

Ryan Field
Tucson, Arizona
November 15, 1942 (in the upper left hand corner is written the letters *H P Y B R H A Y D D* and a note that said, *For Dad – good old pop! Hold up to the light and read.* (Shining through on the other side were the missing letters A P I T D A that spelled, *HAPPY BIRTHDAY DAD*).

Dear Mother, Dad and Nancy,

As you know by now I passed my 30 hour check. I don't think any one but these fellows here know what that means. To look back on it now it's just like your visit here. It seems just as if it hadn't happened.

Now I have 37 hours, with 23 to go. In two more weeks (from Wednesday) I will be saying farewell to another "home" – where to I haven't the slightest idea. There are rumors just as there were at S.A.A.B. With about ten flying days (weather permitting) left it means over two hours a day. It's going to be work up to 50 hours. Then we have acrobatic flying – snap rolls, slow rolls, split S's, loops, Cuban eights etc. I have done most of these with the instructor. All I have learned (but not so good) are spins (diagram of spins) *stalls* (diagram) *(various types) (someone just gave me an apple – some that he had got from home (Washington) and it sure is good – best I've ever tasted for a long time - lazy eights* (diagram) *and chandelles* (diagram).

Those 'horns' I was talking about were speaking tubes that are fastened to the helmet. (He added a drawing on the page of a guy's head with goggles and horns facing up on each side; then an upside down picture of same guy, saying *"unhappy devil"*).

Monday I have my 180 degree landing stage, the same thing as the 90 degree but with one more 90 degree turn with power off, or do you understand?

I wish that Harold (uncle) would get those pictures. I gave a few to D. B. and if I could have those I would like it very much. That's when you get time. I know how it is.

I hope you will get this on Tuesday because I m going to call and I hope you will be home and not riding around in the car.

Love, Bob

VIII Kiss Me Once, and Kiss Me Twice

From our back porch I watched Dad struggling with the lawn mower to cut the three week high grass. Wearing his undershirt with old brown suit pants and a pair of black shoes now covered with grass he wiped his sweaty brow with the back of his hand; then went back to pushing the mower. Dry grass flew past him as he went around and around leaving a square of long blades in the center making prisoners of the few blades left, then with one last shove of the machine they were gone and grass lay even.

Amy, my magic skin doll and I watched him pull weeds around the rose bushes. I wondered what he thought about while he worked.

Putting the garden tools into the shed at the side of the garage, he attached the sprinkler head to the end of the curled up hose, unwound it, stretched it across the yard and laid it on the freshly mown grass. At the spigot he turned the water on full force. Water sprayed out freely from one side of the two holed sprinkler. The other hole obviously clogged.

"I've got to fix that someday," he mumbled as he passed me on the steps and went in through the screen door to the kitchen. I followed Dad inside.

"Mmmm," he said. "Cookies."

A delicious wave of baking smells surrounded the room. One of the rare times that the radio was on, someone was singing, *"Kiss me once and kiss me twice and kiss me once again. It's been a long, long time...."*

"They're for Bob," Mother said. "I couldn't think of anything else to send him, so I made cookies."

"Great idea," Dad said as he passed the tray and cunningly scooped up a cookie. "He'll love them."

Ryan Field
Tucson, Arizona
November 22, 1942

Hello Folks!

I guess that I am going to graduate from primary in spite of all my doubts. But – (especially Pop!) this old saying of "I know you can do "it" as if there is nothing to it doesn't go! There are fellows that haven't made it – and their friends said and thought the same thing – so - please don't say that if I put my mind to anything I can do it. I am almost through primary and that's a long way from graduating from "Advanced" where the boys (notice I didn't say "I") get their commissions. (I won't say "I" until I get <u>there</u>).

Saturday I passed my Army check ride, and even though I passed I didn't do very well, in fact the officer (Lt.) (can't spell) has made me do some deep thinking about my flying.

I am not going to be home for Thanksgiving – nobody is! We will be flying and going to school all that day – Maybe if the Japs would take a few days off I could come home but ...the only hope I have for Christmas – is that I may go to Bakersfield for Basic. But even then the fellows that are there are flying seven days a week – that's day and night. From what I hear Primary is not work compared to Basic.

I still have another civilian check, after that I'll be doing aerobatics. I have been doing a few lately. They sure are fun – snap rolls – slow rolls – vertical reversments, loops and combinations of all of them. Friday I tried a slow roll for the first time by myself (solo). The ship is rolled real slow over on its back and then the controls are brought back on the path which causes the ship to roll over the rest of the way – to right side up. When I tried it I forgot what to do when I got upside down - picture me hanging there by my safety belt. I finally, after gliding upside down for sometime, righted myself – was my face red – from dangling there. It's hard to reach the rudder pedals because your feet want to hang down in front of your face – the floor is up instead of down. (He added a cartoon drawing of himself dangling upside down. Bob often repeated himself probably wanted to make sure he had something to write home about).

A snap roll is almost the same but done much quicker.

Sometimes the B-24's from the field near by come over our territory with not much altitude. Then all the fellows do loops, and all those other things to show off, so when they do come by almost every plane in the sky is going through some of the darndest maneuvers. When any of these aren't done right the plane falls into a spin – and plenty of them do this.

It looks as though I have run out of paper and had to use some left-overs.
That's all for now
Love, Bob
P.S.
Tell Frances (aunt) *that I appreciate her suggestions, but those P.J.'s you got for me are all I need – you know the less I have the easier it is to get around. I really don't know what to say.*
I could use some writing paper – and a - no, I don't know what. Oh yes I haven't an identification bracelet. If I get one with wings on it be sure they are pilot's wings. The name is usually on the front with serial number on the back (19097457).
Now that's a suggeston – not especially for Francis – I don't know what – anything, anybody can think of. (Obviously Mother had asked what they could get him for Christmas and this was his answer).

While Bob was going through his basic training and trying to stay alive doing it, massive riots were going on in downtown Los Angeles between the Mexican Pachucos and the American sailors.

Sailors on shore leave visiting dance halls made fun of the Mexican boys with their pegged pants (zoot suits), big shoulder-padded jackets, wide-brimmed hats, and duck-tailed haircuts. According to the sailors they wore the "drape shape," "reet pleet," "stuff cuff." In turn the pachucos thought the sailors looked funny in their tight bell-bottoms with two rows of buttons up the front and of course, their shaved heads. It was such a commotion that Los Angeles was acclaimed out of bounds for shore leave.

The pachucos were everywhere. Some carried razor sharp butcher knives in their belts or boots, and the girls carried razor blades in their pompadours – we heard. In a fight anyone grabbing them by the hair would regret it. Another war – right in our neighborhood – so close – so scary!

United States Army Air Forces
Ryan Field
Tucson, Arizona   November 29, 1942
Dear Mother, Dad and Nancy,
Only a few more days here, thank goodness. Our new commandant sure has it in for us. Yesterday he told the upper classmen that they didn't realize how lucky they were that they are

leaving in a few days. He said that the underclass was going to be "good" soldiers if it meant no weekend passes for the duration of their stay and drill on Sat & Sunday. He is one of those "90 day wonders", an R.O.T.C. boy from Nebraska. Well enough for him.

I have only four more hours to fly – all my checks are in the past. I have been flying from the front seat to get used to seating up in front. That's where the pilots sit in the B.T.'s (Basic Trainers). We had a demonstration of the basic trainers yesterday. There is no comparison between the P.T.'s and the B.T's. The BT's are closed cockpit, heated, a 450 horse-power and weighs twice as much as the PT's. They have two way radios in them. Their range is 800 miles, enough to fly home. I still don't know where we are going- or when, probably (will know) Wednesday or Thursday.

Flying from the front seat I can talk to my instructor, so I tell him what to do, just as if he were the student. He does it all wrong and I am supposed to correct him – I don't think I'll ever be able to solo him. I am going to recommend him for elimination. Some of the fellows really bawl their instructors out. When we land and get out we talk to the instructor and tell him if he doesn't improve his flying is going to be just too bad.

Love, Bob

p.s. Hi to Nancy

Along with the other aviation cadets, Bob had just completed five months of the six required in primary flight training school. Behind them lay 25 hours of Aptitude flying, problems of interim trainer flying plus classroom flights. Now they had the most tense and exciting moment to look forward to – what kind of plane would they be assigned.

When the transfer came through Bob found himself and most of the members of his squadron moved to Taft, California. The new field was not much different than the others had been. Barracks, planes, Commanders, instructors and cooks all new, but very much the same. The first week was one of turmoil and confusion. The classes began where they had left off and the cadets adjusted quickly to the new routine.

He was told by one of the cadets to expect a very tough instructor. Bob prepared for the worst. He strode across the field where the squadron commander waved a come on. He sized him up as having just passed the height requirement by a fraction of an inch. The commander was wearing his flight suit and carried a clip board. The commander wasted no time in explaining to Bob what he expected

– climbing to 4,000 feet at a 90 degree angle while maintaining 90 mph and an airspeed of 2,100 rpm's.

In the air, Bob listened to the commander's voice coming through his head phones, and followed instructions. His head swiveled around constantly watching for other planes that were going through the same drills, while his other head, the one he wished he had, watched the instrument panel. The air speed indicator started to move off the 90 degree mph mark. Through the interphone system the voice came loud and clear, "Do you know what the instruments are for?"

"Yes sir," was the reply.

"Then use them!"

Bob kept his eyes on the air speed indicator.

"Why are you watching the panel? Keep a look out for planes," came the command.

Bob began the turn when instructed to do so. The instructor's voice blared commands at him and he felt confused. Then he remembered something about a "test under strain and confusion." Of course, that is what the instructor was doing, trying to confuse him. He had to stay calm – ignore the voice.

As he started to bank the plane into another turn, he felt a peculiar sensation. The fuselage was twisting in the opposite direction of the rotation of the propeller. He banked to the right, the wings were level, he banked to the left, the torque seemed to twist and turn to grotesque proportions.

"Counteract with ailerons," came the command.

This time he did not ignore the voice. The plane came straight again, the commander said, "Check for clearance."

"Clearance okay."

"Roll 20 degrees, flaps down, throttle back. Change pitch, roll elevator top back, maintain altitude of exactly 1,050 feet at 2,000 rpm." Bob followed directions. By this time he had learned that the instructors usually meant what they said and he did exactly that.

"Make a 90 degree turn into the field, roll 20 degrees more. Flaps down."

His head switched from right to left, like a cow's tail shooing away flies, watching for other planes. The minutes passed slowly and he could feel the sweat drip behind his ears under the helmet. Then he touched down. Once on the ground, Bob breathed deeply and removed the warm headpiece. He wiped his forehead and tried to control the shaking in his arms caused by tension.

"You did all right," the instructor said, "But learn those instruments well. The advanced trainers have three times as many."

He watched the instructor walk away and wondered if he would ever be able to remember all there was to know about flying. He looked above at the trainers and wondered how a pilot could operate a gun and at the same time fly.

"Amazing isn't it?" A voice beside him said. "I mean, flying. Amazing how a hunk of metal can fly free and easy through the air like a bird."

Bob looked up into the face of a tall cadet standing next to him and nodded in agreement. Carl Baer, a tall fellow with brown bushy eyebrows and wearing a frown, had been one of the new cadets assigned to the same barracks with Bob and Tommy. From the start Carl was hard to know. He was willing, perhaps over zealous with his friendship, pushing, trying to be accepted but something in his make-up was lacking and the others could not take him as one of the 'gang'. When it came to card playing it was obvious that Carl, as a sport, was a poor one. And when flying, the peculiar green pigment expressed on his face was frightening to them all. The cadets were unsure of Carl and preferred to keep their distance. There was nothing really wrong with him except that he was so unsure of himself that the others were afraid it would be contagious.

Bob was one to step forward and defend Carl. "This guy obviously needs someone to help him," he said. "If we can help him overcome whatever it is that makes him the way he is, then it will be easier on all of us living here together. And then in a few weeks we'll graduate with top honors, no doubt, and probably never see the guy again."

Carl confided in Bob when the others were not around. "It's a funny thing about flying," he said. "I get cold feet when it comes to getting in one of those things."

"We all do," Bob told him. "But how did you make it this far if you were really scared?"

Carl shrugged. "Truthfully, I don't know. It was something I wanted to do, and forced myself into but I don't know how long I'm going to be able to keep up."

"Don't worry," Bob said, "just follow the rest of us and if we can make it, then certainly you can. My guess is, you'll be teaching us what to do one of these days." Bob laughed at this to be friendly but also at the absurdity of the idea.

Blackout landings were part of the required tests. Pilot, then acting co-pilot were to take turns flying. First there would be only a few lights lining the field, then only landing lights were permitted and then nothing – just blackness.

As he piloted the plane in the dark he couldn't help but wonder if it was all necessary. Uncontrollable thoughts came to him. "I hope and pray this mess is cleared up before I finish training. Why do I feel this way? I'm no coward. I love to fly and I love peace. Perhaps that's what it's all about. But I'm sure tired."

The thought of having the marvelous flying machines damaged or destroyed in any way or worst still, across the ocean in another world was distasteful and he was glad to feel the contact of earth and plane as it touched down on the black asphalt in the black night.

Once safely landed and after bedding the planes down for the night, the crew sauntered towards the barracks to sleep the remainder of the night.

Carl had gone on ahead of Bob while Tommy caught up with Bob.

"Now I wasn't sure we were going to make that one," he said. "How'd our friend Carl do?"

"He landed okay but I don't think he was very confident. He didn't say a word when we finished, just picked up his gear and cut out across the field."

"Well, I wouldn't worry about him. Next thing you know, you'll be taking his test for him. Just wait and see."

"Ah come on Tex, he's not that bad – maybe."

"Maybe is the word. But I'd rather pick briers off a brier bush than have him in the same cockpit with me. He makes me darned nervous. I can't think which way is up and that could be a catastrophe some day. It's not that he twitches, or wrings his hands or anything like that, just that he sits there so dead quiet. Like a corpse. Then when the instrument panel glows on that white complexion of his, I'm scared to look at him."

"You're exaggerating, "Bob told him.

"Maybe a little, I agree, but not much more than a breath. Man, I hope he gets transferred out of our squadron."

Taft, California
Gardner Field
December 11, 1942
Dear Mother, Dad & Nancy
I hope you are prepared for the shock of receiving a letter.

Saturday night ---(sirens sounded "alert". Now after doing a few things I continue) I wrote letters to everyone but you, as you know. I had planned to write you a long letter but we had to fall out for drill and get flying equipment. Then I was going to phone you, but again more exercises – anyway I am writing a letter now.

Sunday we started school. I have two classes. Navigation and Weather classes are the ones I have now. I am going to have more radio code, aircraft identification and some other short classes.

I started flying Monday, it was just an initiation ride. All I did was a few medium turns and got confused about everything else. The next day my instructor showed me all the stalls (10 in all) spins, climbing and gliding turns, and how to operate some of the new controls.

There are all the controls we had in the Ryan plus a million more. These are the ones that come to mind. There is the stick, rudders, flaps, rudder tab, elevator tab, mixers (carburetor) control, propeller pitch control, throttle, gas tank selector valve, and more. These have to be coordinated to have the instruments read the proper marks. Oh yes, there is the carburetor air heater, oil cooler shutter, cabin heater (ah!) and lots of radio controls. If I stopped to think I could tell you more of them.

Time for lights out. I'll write more later.
Love, Bob

Once a month on Friday or Saturday night, Mother and Dad met with three other couples for Bridge and dessert. They took turns trading off houses. Having no baby sitter I tagged along. Friends my parent's age had older children that entertained me. They took me to their room where we played games and talked. They were all very kind and treated me like one of them. They enjoyed telling stories about their boyfriends. One of them said she was engaged to two sailors and a soldier. How could that be, I wondered? She explained it was her patriotic duty to keep the boys happy that were going off to war to be killed. Another girl asked her what she would do if they all came back at the same time and expected her to marry them. She said she hadn't thought of that.

We were all hoping Bob would be home for Christmas. Preparations were made just in case as he never seemed to know until the last minute. But we unpacked the numerous boxes of ornaments for the tree and the celluloid toys that went under it. Bob was meticulous about how the tinsel was put on – one strand at a time - so we saved that for him in anticipation of his furlough.

The letter head showed an airplane propeller and an air cadet insignia.

Gardner Field
Taft, California
December 12, 1942
Dear Mother, Dad and Nancy

I am waiting for inspection. The floors are mopped, windows washed, shoes polished, room dusted, beds made extra special, and lockers in order. I'm all set – I hope.

I hope to solo, maybe today, but by Monday at the latest.

Our squadron commander is going to ride with every cadet before we solo. I had my ride Tuesday. What a ride. From start to finish he was jumping on me to do this and that! Before we went up he told me to do combing (climbing?) turns up the 4,000ft. These turns were to be 90 degree and the air speed was to be 90 mph. The engine was to be turning at 2,100 r.p.m. I didn't realize that he meant <u>exactly</u> what he said, but I soon found out.

Let me tell you this is a job. My head is supposed to be turning constantly, looking for other planes. So trying to do four of five things at once in an unfamiliar plane is a job. The second the airspeed indicator started to move off 90 M.P.H. the captain would yell at me through the interphone system. He asked me if I knew what the instrument was for, then when I said yes, he told me to use it. Then he said, "Quit looking at the instrument panel," to look around more. Just about that time I would have to start rolling out of the turn, but he would try to keep my mind on other things to see if I would forget about the turn. While doing climbing turns the torque due to the engine makes the plane tend to twist in the opposite direction of rotation of the propeller. This would cause the wings to come level in a right bank, and in a left bank the torque would cause it to become steeper. This is counteracted by using some aileron. I am still confused. This is nothing compared to making an approach to the field and landing.

(If you read this slowly it would give me just enough time to do each one, just as it actually happens). I have to roll 20 degrees of flaps down, throttle back, change pitch, roll elevator tab back (proper amount), maintain an altitude of exactly 1,050 feet at 2,000 rpm make 90 degree turns into the field, roll 20 degrees more flaps down just before landing and always looking for other planes. Going about 120 mph it doesn't take but a few minutes to do all this. I can

remember just what to do when I am on the ground, but when I get up there and start to do it, it has to be done so fast that unless I can do it instinctively – well – it's impossible. I am gradually catching on though. They say that an advanced trainer has three times the gadgets! How about a fighter? It's beyond me how they can do all that and still have time to fly the airplane.

With this plane I could take off here and be over the house within 40 minutes and if you turned your radio on short wave I could talk to you. Sounds good doesn't it? We can pick up the tower radioing to the planes at night directing them into the field.

First the fellows use field flood lights and radio to land at night. Then they use their own landing lights and radio. After that they just use landing lights. Before they graduate they must be able to do "black out" landings. All there is to go by is four lanterns, one at each corner of the run way – sounds exciting doesn't it? Sometimes the night flyers fly over the barracks with the propeller in low pitch. The whole building vibrates all over. Here we are trying to sleep.

To show you how the fellows are concentrating on flying half of them talk in their sleep about some of the mistakes they have made. I woke up a little early this morning and my room mate was going through a spin and pulling out of it. He was talking so loud that he could be heard in the next room.

We are fed like a king or even better considering the situation. Fried and scrambled eggs, sausage, bacon, hot cakes, cocoa, milk, oranges, apples, bananas, hot and dry cereal and more have made up our breakfasts so far. Lunch and dinner are just as good. This is the place if anyone wants to eat. Just found out there isn't going to be an inspection and that I have to fall out for athletics. I'll finish when I get back. –

We have had celery, lettuce, tomatoes, raw carrots, combination salads at dinner and lunch (not all at once). And meat! Thick slices and as may slices as you want. We have had ham, lamb, pork and good fish. To top it off we have pies that are made in our own kitchen. Of course there is always ice cream to go with it.

I can't think of much more. I'll phone you tonight {Saturday}. So until then

Goodbye, love Bob

Hello Nancy – are you already for Christmas? I hope I will be there with you in time to help you open your presents – and mine too – or two. How are you doing in school? It's time for those good lunches I've been telling you about – so – goodbye

Love your Brother

Everyone including Bob was surprised that he got home on Christmas Eve. He was tired. Tired of flying, tired of the same exhausted faces, the drab uniforms, the dusty fields, the bleak barracks. He wanted to be near his family and Dorothy Barbara. The eight foot Christmas tree was decorated and stood in the corner by the front window next to the fireplace. A few wrapped presents sat under it. The fire was lit even though the temperature during the day had been in the 80's. The mahogany table in the dining room was covered with a white linen cloth. In the center sat an arrangement of Poinsettias. White China dishes and the best silver – freshly polished - marked off each place. It was going to be a perfect Christmas Eve; one to remember forever.

The meal preparation took days. Pies had to be made; bread was dried in the oven and crumbled up for stuffing. The turkey was always fresh. The night before I would help clean the bird by picking black pin feathers out of the skin with a tweezers. Then Mother would pull the guts out, cook them and wash the inside thoroughly before stuffing the turkey with dried bread crumbs, celery, walnuts and giblets.

Nothing smelled better than roasting turkey, and nothing tasted better than mashed potatoes and turkey gravy. (Maybe it was just the way she cooked it, or maybe turkeys were better then, but turkey dinners today really don't compare). The whole turkey was brought to the table and Dad carved it, never to Mother's liking of course. "Make thin slices," she would say. Bowls of candied sweet potatoes, mashed potatoes, cranberry sauce, creamed onions, fresh shelled peas, platters of sliced tomatoes, pimiento cheese stuffed celery sticks, lots of olives, bread and butter pickles and a Jell-O salad. Always fresh warm yeast rolls, and for dessert Pumpkin Pie and Mincemeat Pie with whipped cream or hard sauce.

Bob burst into the door shouting, "Hey, anybody home?"

Dorothy Barbara, who had been in the kitchen helping Mother, ran to greet him with a big hug. I dropped the plate of sliced tomatoes I was carrying and didn't know if I should clean it up or greet Bob. Mother decided I should clean it up first.

"What smells so good?" He asked.

"Turkey," Mother answered.

"How did you manage a turkey?"

"Your dad's finagling'," she answered. "He stood in line for two hours at the butcher shop to get it."

"Speaking of turkeys, where is Dad?"

"He's showing my mother around the back yard," Dorathy Barbara told him. "Shall we have a look?"

Dad was overwhelmed to see his son and talked his ear off during dinner. Bob and Dorathy Barbara finished trimming the tree, tossing tinsel on each other's head as if they were little kids. Mom suggested the clean-up be left for later and they open presents. Bob was embarrassed when all the packages were heaped upon him. "Oh, I didn't have time for shopping," he said. "I wasn't even sure I had this leave until yesterday. I do have some of these gold cadet wings, if you want them."

"My boy," Dad said, "Having you home again is the nicest present we would ever hope for."

The 48 hours were up much too soon. Bob returned to the base, a box of fruit cake and cookies tucked under his arm and the deep love he felt for Dorathy Barbara tucked in his heart. He felt light headed and wanted to dance, wave his arms about and shout, "Hooray for life!" but instead he whistled softly as he entered his home away from home.

IX Somewhere Over the Rainbow

Tommy greeted Bob with exciting news. "I asked Blossom to marry me and guess what? She said yes! I'm really happy, man. She's a terrific gal!"

Bob congratulated him and confessed he was a breath away from doing the same thing. Then they both laughed and tears rolled down their cheeks. They didn't know why it struck them as being funny but there they were caught between childhood and the adult world again.

When Carl came in and saw them he wondered if he could be in on the joke. This was even funnier when they explained, that it was not a joke that they were both getting married – that's all. And that struck them as funny too. But their laughter was soon put to rest when they learned they were due on the field in an hour.

One of the guys put his finger glasses upside-down over his eyes, swooped around the room in an imaginary dive making sputtering noises with his tongue lapping the roof of his mouth, then said, "Junior Birdmen to the rescue."

"Not in this fog," Tommy said.

"Regardless Birdmen, we must perform our functions under the hood," said the Birdman. "Blind flying. Nothing like it!" He put his finger glasses back to his eyes. "Shall we go?"

Besides blind flying, the squadron practiced more night flying, cross-country trips, formation flying and a little more acrobatics.

Carl was still having trouble adjusting to military life. Everyone thought he could be a coward as he was often sick on test days. Carl earned the reputation for being a chicken and there was friction between the crew. He had trouble with vertigo and night flying. The whole squadron hoped they would never have to fly anywhere near Carl.

"I don't like this one bit," Tommy said, "Someday, he's going to find a way out of this. Mark my words."

Gardner Field
Taft, California
December 30, 1942
Hello Folks and Nancy,

I am going to try to get some other state to adopt me – this @*!!#* sunny Calif. I was to fly all day yesterday, today and tomorrow – but the fog had some thing else to say about it. I might have gotten off for New Years Day.

I don't know what I'm writing this for, I am going to call you tonight.

I have been flying under the "hood". That's the same as flying blind and using instruments. This thing called "vertigo" proves that human senses and reasoning are wrong. Sometimes I could swear (?) I was turning and climbing when the instruments indicated a straight and level flight. I never have had so many things to watch and think about – and do at the same time.

It was good to get home for Christmas. I don't know when the next trip will be, but soon I hope. Would you thank Mr. Meier (Former Sunday school teacher) for his card when you speak to him again? I wrote to Herman (uncle) and thanked him for his present. I received some candy covered nuts from Alice (aunt). She didn't have any return address on it so....would you do the honors for me or give me her address?

I don't know much more to say that I'm not going to say tonight

Love Bob

Boy! Did I eat tonight! (His drawing was a stick man with a protruding stomach).

The boys did a lot of thinking about what would happen to them when the war was over. The discussion brought up the subject of the number of pilots flying in the air force. If the entire United States Air Force was going to turn out pilots and airplane technicians – a half million men and they all wanted to work for commercial airlines, they said, what chance would they have for a job?

Bob put in that he didn't believe they would all choose flying for a profession. *"Some already have jobs waiting for them at home and there will be plenty of jobs opening up when everyone is home again."* In fact he was looking forward to returning to the designing jewelry in Hollywood for the movie stars.

Mother took good care of her mother, who lived with us. Then one day Grandma died. The door to Grandma's bedroom was closed. Some men in dark suits came to the house to take grandma away. Mother urged me to go outside and play. She was very kind about it, but I knew something was wrong. Something was going on that I wasn't supposed to know about. Quietly I sneaked around to the bedroom window. Standing on a faucet-fitting I boosted myself up so I could see, but the shade was pulled down. For a long time I sat on the grass under the walnut tree thinking of Grandma, who was a dear to me. Only a few days earlier she had been sitting at her sewing machine making a dress for me while listening to her favorite soap operas – *"As the World Turns"* and *"Stella Dallas."*

The house was quiet without Grandma or Bob while out there, across the ocean was a raging war. Children like me were dying. It was terrifying just to think about it. I wished the war would end.

Bob phoned home on January 20th to wish me a happy birthday – my ninth.

Taft, California
January 26, 1943
Dear Mother, Dad and Nancy,

Well, I passed my 40 hour and instrument check and have been running ragged. I've been on the flight line all day for the past 6 days. Tuesday we went on a 300 mile cross-country which took about 2 ½ hours. The next day was the instrument check which was 30 minutes under the hood trying to do turns and lots more all in the bumpiest weather I've been in. Then on our day off it rained all day.

We've been flying for 40 hour check at low ceiling 6,000 feet. I spent most of my time dodging planes. And straight off we had blackout landings. And it was black. Clouds covered the sky. After the 40 hour check I flew solo formation for 1 hour, then 2 more hours of formation followed by acrobatics. I have 66 ½ hours which leaves 3 ½ to go. 2 hours of that is night cross-country to Madera and back 290 miles. I'm really looking forward to that!

We're scheduled to leave here on the 3rd or 4th. They asked our choice of "twin engine" or "single engine" advanced training schools. I took twin engine but it doesn't mean I'm going to get it.

Love, Bob

The transfer came and Bob was sent to Armed Air Corps Advanced Flying School in Texas.

Marfa, Texas

February 11th, 1943
Dear Folks and Nancy,

I've not only "got a bit of Texas in my walk; there's quite a bit of it in my eyes, ears, hair, shoes etc, etc. Sand, dust, dust, dust and yes! More dust everywhere. There are some P.S. (previous service) men in our squadron. They all agree that they have never seen such a post as this. The upper-classmen are counting the days they have left – so are we.

Our barracks are small, one story, cement floor. Oh well, we have a small stove that burns COAL! (Drawing of stove) *the rooms are wide enough for a bed to squeeze into (3 inches left over at each end) and about 18 feet long – with four to a room. The walls including the outside wall are one thickness of fire board.* (Drawings of room and barracks). *These buildings have hooks on the sides with stakes in the ground along side so that when the wind blows stronger than usual they may be roped down. I have never felt it so far.*

We fly AT-17's (Advanced trainers) *for the first 35-40 hours, then fly AT-9's (like on the letter head) that's the only thing that I am looking forward to, besides, leaving here. The AT-17's are those wooden crates – nobody enjoys flying them, especially in BUMPY air – (usual conditions). But the AT-9's are really airplanes. They have one of the greatest wing loadings (weight of ship compared to the area of the wing) for real small wings and very heavy wings and fuselage) – of any ship, even combat ships. They cruise at 180 mph and land at 120 mph. A P-38 lands at 110 mph. That's all I think about flying – the AT-9 and not the "Balsa Bomber" or AT-17.*

I don't have much time to myself. I get back from the flight line at 6:30 and then eat. By the time I finish dinner its 7:30. That only leaves 2 ½ hours to study, write letters, clean up and get ready for bed. Taps at 10:00.

Some that graduated the day we arrived were sent to an observation unit. They will fly stripped down P-38's, no guns, no armor plate, just speed. They will be mounted with a special camera for observation purposes. I sure would like to get that. No shooting just low flying and fast. But then again I might be flying a B-24 or a Flying Fortress. I hope not. These Cessna's are not good but they have the same amount of switches, instrument and controls that any twin engine ship has. It's a job to fly and make all the instruments register properly. There are so many things to check – even before taking off - that we have a list. There are 49 things to check before take off.

I wonder how you are doing with your gas station, Dad, or have you still got it? Hope you're making out alright. And how is Rosie? You ought to see the rudder pedals in these flying bath tubs B-17. Nothing is any good.

Love, Bob

Dad had purchased a gas station in hopes of making a decent wage but he didn't know how to run it. The hired help were either too young or too old and didn't earn their keep. Dad worked 12 to 14 hours a day and still didn't make ends meet. He was grateful to sell it, but then he was out of work again.

From January to March training schedules were tightened. It was flying, schooling, studying, eating, and sleeping over and over again. The cadets learned about bombs and bombing, how to read maps and aerial photographs and how to clean the desert out of the barracks. They ate what they called 'dog biscuits' and drank 'chlorinated water.' They trained on PT-22, Primary Trainers; AT-7, Advance Trainers; P-39, Fighter and the Boeing B-17, Flying Fortress Bomber and the B-29, Super Fortress. Tired and sore from vigorous exercises, then flying and flying and flying, it was a temptation to give up – wash out – quit. And where was Carl all this time? In the infirmary – resting. Carl had to make up his time but only the flying part – not the field exercises. (One wonders?)

The letter head this time showed three planes flying with twin engines. Next to the picture he wrote – *AT-9 not AT-17 that I am flying at present.*

Marfa, Texas

March 5, 1943

Dear Mother, Dad, and Nancy –

I am sorry that I can't answer your letter sooner – and Nancy's letter. I am glad that you are doing well in school. I am still going to school learning about bombs, bombing and how to read maps and aerial photographs.

The wind is really blowing. This morning it was calm – then before noon it's going over 40 miles an hour. I sweep the floor and 10 minutes later it's covered with sand.

I went up this morning and had to land in the wind when I came down. Let me tell you it's a job to land one of these 'kites' in a 40 mph cross wind. After landing, the engines are used to steer the plane. If you want to turn left, the right engine is speeded up to make the turn. When the plane is going (on the ground) with the wind blowing from one side, the airplane has a definite tendency to turn into the wind. Then the opposite engine is used to keep the ship from turning. The wind got so strong that the one engine was running at full power to keep going straight. When it (the wind) gets like this the plane can't take off – so no more flying (that day).

I will be an unpperclass man next Tuesday – for the last time. When I graduate (April 12) I will be known as a "Junior Birdmen" for quite sometime. I don't care what they call me as long as I get out of this place. I suppose that there are a few oasis, like in a desert, in Texas that are alright – but from what I've seen, they should give it back to Mexico. In the last three days I have flown over 1,000 miles – all of it in Texas. I have been going on cross countries. Even though this is desolate, barren land (population 1 ½ persons per square mile) it is impressive to fly over it (when it isn't bumpy). I have been over the Rio Grande several times. It isn't much of a river, but it is down in a large, deep valley –something like the Grand Canyon without colors and not such a definite drop.

It's almost time for school. I just had lunch in the new cadet mess hall. It just opened today. Up until now we have been on field rations. After Gardener Field it's like bread and water, and bad water at that. It sure will be good to taste some water that hasn't been chlorinated. I should be tell you about flying instead of about this –

Yesterday I went before the board, as all cadets do before they are commissioned. There you tell them what you want to be assigned to after you graduate. They have your record before them and they look you over and recommend – or disapprove your becoming an officer – and your choice on the assignment. I asked for (three choices) 1st, P-38 Observation, that is photographing objectives before and after bombing (time out for school)......

This is a new type of observation made possible by new cameras for fast flying planes. I doubt if I will get it, but I asked. My 2nd choice was a B-26 Combat – that's a Martin medium bomber with the speed of most fighters. The last choice was Douglas A-20 Combat. Now all I have to do is wait. At last that feeling of suspense and worry about being washed out is disappearing – maybe it's because of this place creating a feeling of indifference – it's not as bad as that.

Tuesday night I start night flying. I will finish my day flying and ground school about a week from Tuesday. Then all I will have is night flying, athletics and some skeet shooting.

I don't have much time to write. From the time I get up until about 7:15 I am doing something. From 7:15 until 10 the time really goes fast. The time is going by faster than I have ever seen it – this is the end of the forth week! Soon it will be the fifth – sixth – seventh etc. The less time there is the faster it goes – so it won't be long.

I hope you, - Mother and Dad, are getting along with your jobs.

So long,
Love, Bob

P.S. I suppose there are some questions that I should have answered but if I read your letters again, I won't have enough time.

P.S.S. Dad I hope you don't exaggerate the capabilities of my airplane. I m still flying 'the Family Car of the Air' (speed 140 mph).

P.S.S.S. Please deposit money in bank. Ah, yes, take $3.00 out for flowers – or whatever it costs. (For Dorothy Barbara).

The days flew and the cadets flew. Concentration was high and morale low. There was little time for thoughts other than what they should know to pass the tests. Some even dreamed about it.

"Roll – pitch – pull stick back – stick back!"

Bob rolled over on his bunk and shook Tommy in the next bed. "Wake up! You can't fly in your sleep."

Marfa, Texas
March 14, 1943
Sunday
Dear Mother, Dad and Nancy,
Thank you very much for the cookies. They arrived in good condition – and are disappearing fast.

Only four more weeks! I just finished ground school today, so from now on all I will have is skeet shooting, athletics, link trainer, drill (ever other day) and night flying. I have almost finished all the day flying unless I get some time in an AT-9 (I hope). The schedule has been so mixed up that I/we don't know what I/we are/am to do from one hour to the next. This morning I had three hours of school, 8:00 to 11:00 and tonight I will fly from 7:00 until 2:00 in the morning. Then tomorrow night I will fly the same hours again – I could go to sleep right now without even trying.

Night flying here is entirely different than at Gardner Field.

There aren't any zones to fly in – no boundaries at all. We are to make at least four landings each night, then after that we have formation – or just go where we please. I have never had so much fun as I have had flying at night. Of course we have to look around more to see if anybody is around but the navigation lights are easily seen. There is a red light on the left wing, a green one on the right and a white one on the tail. One night last week when I was flying I saw about five sets of lights coming my way, they weren't in formation, but one behind the other. As they passed me I turned and joined in. Soon there were more fellows who added on to the end. Here we were playing follow the leader. When we were going straight and level I could only see a few white lights in front of me. Then when the first one would turn I would see one light after another turning and following the line. That was fun. When, at 2:00 (a.m.), all the planes are coming back home at the same time makes it quite congested.

Friday I was up before sunset and I watched the shadows lengthen and the darkness fill up the Rio Grand Valley. It's not at all like the sunrise. Watching the sunrise gives me such a clean refreshed feeling but the sunset creates a relaxed feeling while I change from one world to another. The moon hasn't been very bright and it's hard to see any clouds that might be up there. The first thing you know the stars and light disappear – then you really are alone – (in these ships you always have a co-pilot, we take turns being pilot and co-pilot). There aren't any lights inside of the plane except a fluorescent light which gives off a deep violet color that can hardly be seen. This light causes the phosphorescent, or radium faces on the instruments to glow. They seem to stand out so that you could reach out and pick each number out of the air. These numbers glow just like those rocks with the radio active chemicals in them when as ultra-violet light is turned on them, just like the ones at Knott's Berry Farm and the Planetarium at Griffith Park. So there I am in complete blackness (wondering if some one is coming the other way) (but the chances are a million to one that there isn't anyone coming) flying instruments until I emerge and can see a faint horizon.

I hope that you – Ma and Pa are getting along alright – and Nancy is getting good grades at school.

So long,
Love, Bob

Knott's Berry Farm was a popular place for us to visit with their special recipes for fried chicken, biscuits with boysenberry jam, mashed potatoes and gravy, rhubarb, and of course boysenberry pie.

(This was and still is a delicious place to eat. Now with an amusement park attached, it is a focus point for entertainment in the Orange County area). (And the Griffith Park Planetarium has recently, in 2006, been renovated, updated and even better than it was in the 1940's. A huge fire in 2007 came dangerously near the site).

Marfa, Texas
March 23, 1943
Dear Folks and Nancy,

Only 20 more days, then I will no longer be an Aviation Cadet.

Yesterday morning I received all my flying equipment that I will be using for the duration. I have my own parachute, a piece of nylon 24 feet in diameter (not one single piece) which I will carry with me wherever I go. I have a summer flying suit and a winter flying suit. The summer suit is a dark green jumper with plenty of zippers – a cap comes with this too. Ah! The winter suit is something I should have had for riding the motorcycle. Top to bottom (feet) it is: one fleece lined helmet, one fleece lined leather jacket, one fleece lined leather pair of pants and a pair of fleece lined leather-rubber boots and gloves to match.

My silhouetted (oh! oh!) shadow looks like Man Mountain Dean's when I have all this on. Then I also have an oxygen mask and a nice bright yellow 'vest type' life preserver. To inflate this all I have to do is pull a chord and two small metal flasks fill with carbon dioxide, CO/2 fills the jacket. To put all this equipment in I have a parachute bag and a big zipper bag. I can put all my flying equipment and the parachute in the parachute bag. The other bag (more bags!) is for uniforms when it is unfolded pants, blouses and shirts can be hung up. Then it is folded and zipped – all the clothes are kept unwrinkled. There are big pockets (zipper) on the sides for other things. Of course I can't get all my clothing in these two bags ...... (I also got a wool sweater and a leather jacket) – and glasses and goggles – etc.

I have been pretty busy since I have become an upper classmen (for the last time). Reveille is at 05:15 now and I won't be in bed until 0300 tomorrow morning. Just 22 hours of work. To make up for the loss of sleep we 'sleep in' until 9:15. When we get up we rush to make our beds and clean up the room – then to athletics (still asleep) – what a life. Then lunch followed by an hour of drill. We don't mind this, everyone drills even the officers including the colonel! Then we fly in the afternoon until 7:30. By the time we finish *dinner it is 8:30. This leaves 1 ½ hours – and it goes <u>FAST</u>!!!*

The next day we have lectures on Military Courtesy etc., athletics, drill, link trainer and miscellaneous things that must be taken care of. Today we have two hours for which something wasn't scheduled, so, as all good little boys, we have two hours of "study hall." Captain O'Connor, the Director of Ground School was President of a Junior High School – and runs this place the same way. When he doesn't get his way, he comes so close to crying that his eyes begin to water. He should be home knitting for the Red Cross where he would do the war effort some good instead of demoralizing the cadets. How some of these P.H.'s ("Pin Heads," as one of our teachers calls him) get to be officers is beyond me. {And the other cadets). The time isn't wasted, we get to read the latest confidential and secret reports on the different campaigns. To read these - and then the newspapers – well it's like the time that Topanga Canyon was on fire. From what the paper said, it was all on fire. But when we got there the papers were wrong. It's the same old thing, the papers tell the public what they want so they give good things in head-lines and bad things in small print or not at all. – I'm not predicting the end of the things but if it ends within 3 or 4 years plenty of people will be surprised.

I have over 60 hours pilot time and an equal amount of co-pilot time. This means that I will have well over 200 hours (counting Primary and Basic) when I graduate. Saturday afternoon I had a cross-country with a minimum and maximum altitude of 500 feet above the ground – all the way. Of course it's hard to judge 500 feet above ground you haven't been over before, besides my instructor said it was alright to go as low as we wanted to, so long as we didn't go out of our way to buzz anything – and not to buzz people or houses. It finally ended up with three of us flying formation (not to be done unless an instructor is in one of the planes) over a railroad. We passed over a <u>small</u> town – and a passenger train was stopped there and every body was out looking around. We didn't see them until we were over them (about 30 feet) which was too late – too bad but we didn't feel sorry for them. I never saw such a bunch of bewildered faces in all my life. At 30 feet above the ground going 160 M.P.H. they didn't know what to think. Low flying is about the only way a person gets a sensation of speed – and what a sensation.

Yesterday I was flying formation with my instructor, who was in another ship, and we did some more buzzing. It sure is fun around these mountains and canyons. These are about the only times that I have done any buzzing. It will probably be the last, all the rest of our time will be high altitude cross countries (x-c) exercises) *(10,000 – 11.500 feet)*. Tonight I am going to El Paso, but without stopping. Later on this week I am going to Douglas Arizona and after that Albuquerque, New Mexico. These will be day-night x-c, start in the day and end sometime during the night.

This is the first real chance to write I've had. I am sure I will have more time next week (I hope).

I got a letter from Charles Legrand. He sends his regards. He can't say much, where he is or what he is doing. He is still in Alaska. The letter was airmail. It was sent to Tucson – to Taft and finally here. It only took five days to get here from the day it was post marked. Quick service!

Well so long

Love Bob

P.S. I guess D.B. told you that I have to the dentist. I am now missing an upper right tooth next to the wisdom tooth. It took 50 minutes to get out, you should have seen the poor dentist work. It couldn't be saved – there wasn't much left.

(This was an 8 page letter. Imagine him spending his precious down time to write this much information home. It took 50 minutes for me to type it from the hand printed original. How long did it take <u>him</u> to write it?)

Bob referred to a cabin in Topanga Canyon that the family owned. It was a special retreat that the relatives shared. Near Malibu it seemed like a very long drive to me but actually wasn't far from Los Angeles. The road wound around curves. We chugged up hill until we reached an access road which narrowed and went straight up at such an angle that the car had to be backed up three times to make the turn. All the passengers got out and walked up the hill as it seemed much safer that way. Without the load, the car still strained in low gear jerkily to get up the hill, then had to be parked on the gravel shoulder with wheels turned in and rocks placed behind each tire so the car would not roll down again. Everyone sighed with relief when the engine was finally turned off and the car parked.

The air was fresh and clear in the mountains. Nestled in a heavily wooded and overgrown area, the cabin could not be seen from the road. We had to make our way through the bushes, pushing them aside, hopping on stones over a creek that ran through the property, until we finally reached the wooden porch. This took many trips with bags of groceries and blankets and suitcases. The cabin was just one big room with a large stone fireplace and wrap-around windows that showed a gorgeous view of the valley. A long picnic table with bench seats sat under the windows. There were no bedrooms just two pull down double beds coming out of the wall. Off to one side was a very small kitchen with a sink, water pump and wood burning stove. In the back of the cabin was an outhouse for a toilet. I was so frightened of the spiders and snakes and whatever other surprises might be waiting out there that I held my need to go until the very last minute.

X He Wears a Pair of Silver Wings

Bob became an officer on April 12, 1943. A graduation notice arrived in the mail.

The Marfa Army
Air Forces Advanced Flying School
Marfa, Texas
Announces the graduation of
Class 43 D
Pilots
On Monday morning, April Twelfth
Nineteen hundred and forty-three
Marfa Air Force Base

Inside was a card with his name, Robert C. Remple
    Lieutenant Army Air Force
    United States Army

After graduation, the new officers removed the wire grommet from their caps and titled them at a rakish angle, giving them a Clark Gable look like he had in the movies. The new gold lieutenant bars glittered in the sunshine. Bob had made it and he was proud. The bad news was he was to be a co-pilot on a B-17 – "Flying Fortress" – a four-engine, long range, heavy bomber, as big as a house, or so it seemed to him at the time. After 200 hours of flying, he was to be a "truck driver" in the sky! And the worst possible thing happened. Carl was assigned to be his pilot. Is it any wonder Bob felt second best? How did Carl pass him up when he had missed half the training?

While Carl sat at the controls, Bob went through the checklist before take-off.

The checklist for starting the B-17F was incredible and seemed to take forever to read off but very necessary for safety. The cockpit was crowded with instruments and not much room to move around. Pilot and co-pilot sat close together. "Check list," says the pilot. The co-pilot gets out the printed form.

1. CHECK FORM 1A
2. "GEAR SWITCH?" Asks the co-pilot
3. "NEUTRAL," answers the pilot
4. "FUEL TRANSFER VALVES AND pump?"
5. OFF
6. HYDRAULIC PRESSURE?
7. OK
8. HYDRAULIC SELECTION – NORMAL. INTERCOOLERS – COLD, HAND PRIMER – OFF, PARKING BRAKE – ON.
9. COWL FLAPS
10. OPEN RIGHT, OPEN LEFT
11. CARBURETOR AIR FILTERS
12. OPEN
13. FUEL SHUT-OFF SWITCHES
14. OPEN
15. BOOSTER PUMPS?
16. ON
17. SUPERCHARGERS?
18. OFF
19. THROTTLES?
20. CLOSED
21. PROPELLERS?
22. HIGH RPM
23. AFCE?
24. OFF
25. RADIO COMPASS?
26. OFF
27. FLIGHT CONTROLS?
28. UNLOCKED AND CHECKED
29. CALL CLEAR
30. CLEAR LEFT, CLEAR RIGHT
31. MASTER SWITCH?
32. ON
33. IGNITION SWITCHES?
34. ON
35. BATTERY SWITCHES?
36. ON
37. GENERATOR SWITCHES?
38. OFF
39. INVERTER?

40. ON, ALTERNATE CHECKED
41. FUEL QUANTITY?
42. SUFFICIENT
43. FIRE EXTINGUISHER SELECTOR ON #1 ENGINE
44. START #1 ENGINE, HAND PRIME IF NECESSARY
45. OIL PRESSURE?
46. COMING UP
47. START #2, #3, #4 ENGINES

BEFORE TAXYING OUT
1. RADIO?
2. ON
3. MIXTURE CONTROLS?
4. AUTORICH
5. WING FLAPS?
6. CHECKED
7. TRIM TABS?
8. SET FOR TAKE-OFF
9. GYROS?
10. UNCAGED AN SET
11. ALTIMETER?
12. SET
13. CREW REPORT
14. "ABOARD, SIR."
15. RADIO CALL
16. WHEEL CHOCKS OUT RIGHT, SAYS THE CO-PILOT
17. OUT LEFT
18. TAIL WHEEL – UNLOCKED BRAKES – STANDING BY

BEFORE FIRST TAKE-OFF
1. BRAKES UNLOCKED
2. MAGNETOS
3. CHECK (WITH ENGINES AT 1500 RPM, PUT TURBOS ON, RUN PROPS THRU, RETURN TO HIGH RPM)
4. ENGINES?
5. RUN UP
6. FLIGHT CONTROLS
7. UNLOCKED, FREE
8. TRAIL COWL FLAPS
9. BOOSTER PUMPS ON

10. RADIO CALL -TO TOWER FOR PERMISSION TO TAKE OFF
11. BRAKES?
12. STANDING BY
13. ON RUNWAY: TAIL WHEEL LOCKED GENERATORS

The pilot grasps the control wheel and firmly with his left hand, with his right he moves four throttles forward and the Flying Fortress lifts into the air.

And there was just as many items before landing and on the runway and subsequent take-offs. (How did they do it?)

AFTER TAKE OFF
1. LANDING GEAR – PILOT'S SIGNAL
2. SUPERCHARGERS – PILOT'S SIGNAL
3. PROPELLERS – FOLLOW THROTTLES
4. COWL FLAPS: ADJUST 205 MAX TEMP
5. GEAR SWITCH NEUTRAL (WHEELS UP)
6. BOOSTER PUMPS OFF

Bob and Dorothy Barbara were secretly married soon after he graduated. No one knew except Mother, and she could not keep a secret if her life depended on it. Even without actually saying the words – that they were married – anyone could tell by the look on her face that something romantic was going on. She would not say yes or no, but only hint that Dorothy Barbara had gone to Marfa, Texas for the weekend to visit with Bob. It wasn't hard to figure out that when a single unchaperoned girl goes from Los Angeles to Texas to visit a single boy, that something is going on that no one can talk about openly.

And when Dorothy Barbara returned she was even more giggly and absolutely beaming and grinning from ear to ear. Dad kept mentioning the twinkle in her eyes and she would wink at him. Who were they keeping the secret from? Was it her mother? Did it have something to do with the army? Was he not supposed to marry until after he was commissioned? Why was it such a secret? Dorothy Barbara came back after the weekend, back to her mother's house as if nothing had ever changed.

Dorothy Barbara had a couple of brothers that loved to dance and so did I. One of the brothers, Sonny, who was 17 and had dimples, taught me to jitterbug and we danced in their living room to the recordings of Glenn Miller –*Tuxedo Junction, In the Mood, Chattanooga Choo Choo, String of Pearls* and *Blue Moon*.

On weekends I went with Dorothy Barbara and Sonny to Manhattan Beach where we swam and turned acrobatics in the sand – somersaults, cartwheels and handstands. Sonny would hold me over his head by my hip bones while I balanced myself arms held out to the side, legs straight out behind me and toes pointed, like a Great Blue Heron in flight. We laughed and sang songs: *"I'd rather have a paper doll that I can call my own. A doll that other fellows cannot steal. And all those flirty flirty guys with their flirty flirty eyes will have to flirt with dollies that are real. At night when I come home she will be waiting. She'll be the sweetest doll in all the world. I'd rather have a paper doll, to call my own, than have a fickle-minded real live girl."* We were doing our best to forget the war.

Romance seemed to ooze out of the pores of the earth. Any man wearing a uniform was a hero off to fight for our country. Women joined the USO serving donuts and coffee to sailors and soldiers on leave. There was a lot of singing, dancing, joking and an underlying sadness for not everyone was going to make it back home.

Movie stars marched off to serve in one way or another. Some participated in entertaining the troops, making public appearances at rallies for selling War Bonds. They washed dishes, served food, danced with lonely G.I.'s in the Hollywood Canteen, worked for the Red Cross, and made patriotic movies. *Swing Shift Maize* was a comedy that we related to since Mother was working the swing shift. And *The Human Comedy*, based on a book by William Saroyan and starring Mickey Rooney, who played Homer, made a huge impression on me. It was a story of a young boy whose father had died and his older brother had joined the army. Homer worked at a telegraph office delivering wires from the War Department announcing the deaths of sons on the battlefield. One day a telegram comes announcing the death of his own brother. He tries desperately to cope with his loss and through the struggles hears the words, "You are what we're fighting the war for. You are what we have left behind – to live the hopes we only dreamed." I cried and prayed this wouldn't happen to us.

And of course Bob Hope entertained the troops wherever they were – in the jungle and on board ships. He was with the USO (United States Organization} shows. Betty Grable became the number one pin-up girl in the nation. Servicemen had her picture pinned inside their lockers. Before the day's duty they would kiss their hand and slap it on Betty's backside for luck. Just the pleasure of looking at the blonde beauty in swim suit and beautifully shaped legs was enough for most. Lana Turner made the pull-over sweater a popular fad and every young woman wished to have a bust like the actress.

How I wished I was old enough to be part of the USO and help cheer up the servicemen. But I didn't need to go anywhere. It was as if Mother read my thoughts, for she began bringing servicemen home for Sunday dinner. Soon Sunday's took on another shape. On the way home from church, Mother would spot a hitch hiker in uniform, make Dad pull over and pick him/them up. If they were nice young men, which they all were, she'd invite them home for a home-cooked meal. These young men, barely eighteen some of them, would jump at the chance.

While she would be in the kitchen preparing the meal, I would lounge on the floor with a sailor or soldier and read the Sunday funny paper. This was great fun and no doubt would have continued if she hadn't walked into the living room and found a young sailor with his arm around me, my dress hiked up in the back and my long legs exposed. It was then she realized I was growing up and looking much older for my age than I was.

After that she was very careful who she invited home.

XI I'll Be With You in Apple Blossom Time

Everyone had war fever. Death was in every neighborhood. The future was only dreams away. "Live for today, for tomorrow may never come," was the motto. All I wanted to do was grow up and have peace. I was getting tired of the war. The Movietone News was full of devastating and sad stories. It showed bombed out buildings, homeless people, and starving children. Magazines, newspapers and news reports were only full of bad news. The only good news was that penicillin, an antibiotic, had been discovered from mold found on cantaloupe. This new discovery was believed to save many a soldier's life.

Bob was still disappointed about the plane he was assigned. He wanted something small that he could pilot himself. And he was disappointed that Carl was a First Lieutenant and would be the pilot and he would fly with him as his co-pilot.

Bob wrote home asking Mother to pick out – what they laughingly referred to as an engagement ring for Dorothy Barbara. So the two women went together to select a full carat solitaire for $300. Bob was a little shocked at the price since that was more than he had made in a month but he was glad Dorothy Barbara got what she wanted and made arrangements to pay his mother $67 a month until the ring was paid for.

He was later transferred to Dyersburg, Tennessee.

Tennessee
May 20, 1943
Dear Mother, Dad and Nancy,
I wish that I might see you. It would be so much better saying these things than trying to write them.
Dad, do you remember the day when we were all together at Gardner Field. We had just left the P.X. when you asked me if I was ever going to do anything about Dorothy Barbara. You seemed happy then, when I told you that some day, sometime that – well, any way it's about to happen. I hope you still feel the same.

I wonder how you feel Mother? I know it's not the way you would want it, I feel the same, but what other way could there be? I know you and Dad are happy but Dorothy Barbara's mother - ? It's too bad I can't be there?

How are you going to like your new sister, Nancy? I think she is a pretty nice girl, don't you?

I just talked to Dorothy Barbara, (Remple) (sounds different) she sure sounded excited, not that it doesn't affect mmme (see!). Tom and I have rented two rooms in a house near by. They have been made out of a large room in the attic. It's not as nice as it could be but we can fix them up without much trouble. They are large rooms though. I suppose we could have – or still get a better place (not that this isn't nice) but it's the closest house to the field and we were <u>VERY</u> fortunate to find this place. (Drawings of layout).

It's only a five minute walk from my hut to the house, s-o-o-o Tommy and I plan to move. Some how I happened to find a bunch of pass blanks in my hand just as I left the orderly room, h-m-m-m? Of course if I am ever in a hurry I can jump over the fence.

When you write to me tell me how much I owe you. Dorothy Barbara said that the ring cost $300, with or without tax? I probably owe you about $200. From now on my monthly income will be $328.50. Right now my financial status is not so good (telephone calls etc.) say that I owe you $200 (maybe more or less) would it be alright if I paid you $67 the first of this month and $67 each of the following two months? A lot has to come out of the $328.50 – like food, rent, transportation. Well I guess you have been married long enough to know. Now you let me know how you want it. I imagine you would like to have it all as soon as possible now that you are going to fix up the corner house. I hadn't planned on spending more than $200 on a ring, but it's something that's once in a life time and she will wear it so I am glad that she is happy with what she wanted. Please tell me if you need all of it at once. I could probably borrow some money from some of the boys without much trouble – so let me know.

The country side is really beautiful. Everything is green. Trees are as thick as blades of grass in a lawn. You know I have never seen fire flies until one night on the train when passing through Arkansas. I couldn't figure out what was causing those sparks. I thought it might be caused by sparks from the train, but it finally dawned – they were fire flies. There are a lot of them around here. It sure is pretty to see them, faintly at first, just as the sunsets. Then as if grows darker the little blue spark becomes brighter. I wonder if Dorothy Barbara has ever seen any? Maybe I could try to send some home in a bottle for Nancy? I don't suppose they would work there if they survived the trip.

I have been up once since I have been here. We are terribly short on planes. This is probably good news for you. Pop – it makes our schedule longer. It doesn't make me mad either.

I still am unhappy about "truck driving". I would give ANYTHING TO FLY AN AIRPLANE AGAIN, LIKE AN A-20 OR P-35. Three of my fellow co-pilots took a four day pass, they were so disgusted. One has been court-martialed and the other two are going to be. The sentence for the first one is confinement to the post and fining him his flight pay for one year. At $75 a month. That's almost $1000 for the year or $250 for each day that he was AWOL

Well, good-night
Bob

An officer now, he and Dorothy Barbara could have a proper wedding in Tennessee. With suitcase packed complete with a white gown folded in reams of tissue paper, shoes and veil, along with something old, something new, something borrowed, something blue and not to be forgotten a penny in the shoe, she went by train and was greeted by open arms from Bob and lots of sticky warm weather. But of course she didn't care. They were together. And they were deeply in love.

The wedding was in a small chapel on the base. Tommy was Bob's best man and Blossom was the Matron of Honor, as they were married earlier in Texas. Blossom helped Dorothy Barbara to dress in the white satin gown with hundreds of small covered buttons up the back. It was humid in Tennessee and too warm for a satin gown, but it would have to be.

The exterior of the Chapel was barren of any shrubbery and resembled any ordinary barracks except for the peaked roof. Inside the wood floor creaked beneath the slow methodical steps of the bride. The pews were empty except for a few rows of service men. The bride and groom joined hands and knelt in prayer on the bare wood step in front of the altar. After the kiss that sealed the contract they left the Chapel under a canopy of raised swords held up by the crew from Bob's squadron. From the photographs they sent, Bob looked very happy and I was happy for him.

The honeymoon was only two days but enjoyable as they rested on the mossy bank of Realfoot Lake. Bob, Tommy and

Blossom had cleaned out an attic room in Mrs. Iris' house and made it as cheerful as possible. The place was not without its peculiarities. Thin walls prohibited much privacy from either side and only a two burner electric plate that even an experienced cook, which D.B. was not, would have difficulty preparing an appetizing meal for even an experienced husband, which Bob was not. Consequently most all meals were eaten on the post. Blossom and Tommy were often their dinner partners. Then the two husbands would be off and the wives would be left to dwindle away the hours until their loved ones returned.

When Bob returned he was often so exhausted the sight of the bed beckoned him and he would beg for just five minutes of rest. D.B. spent many evenings just watching him sleep. When he did awaken he would apologize but she didn't mind. She just loved being with him.

Soon they found better accommodations in the home of Mr. and Mrs. Daws, giving them more room in the front of the house. Mrs. Daws was a nice motherly type and offered to drive them into Memphis when they needed a ride.

(This is a letter from Dorothy Barbara and Bob)
Dyersburg, Tennessee
June 4, 1943
Dear Mother, Dad and Nancy,

We're still on our honeymoon. This phase is Realfoot Lake. The lake was formed by an earthquake. Trees grow right in the middle – groves of them! We're on a 2-day pass. It's cool and very lovely here. (Bob interjected, "Don't you believe it"). The cabins are of stone, most attractive. Much like Big Bear at home.

Yesterday we went rowing and came home more than a little damp and sunburned. We're going fishing or swimming this afternoon. As soon as some of the excitement subdues we will write you a connected letter.

Hello folks!

I have been fortunate all these days. But from now on it's not going to be as pleasant as it has been. More work and less play, I'm afraid. I received your package and two letters, but haven't had the time to write. I wish that we could be spending these days in L. A.

We're going swimming if we can find a way to get 6 miles from here – no transportation!

Although I am making more (money), I haven't received any of it yet. My checks will be late this month which makes it *difficult – temporarily. Sure do appreciate the postponement of the "foreclosure" of the $150. By next month everything will be straightened out and running smoothly. We'll write later. This time is valuable. We are having a good time. My wife is such a lovely girl.*

Love, Bob and Dorothy Barbara

Mother was growing weary of the noisy rivet guns, of the rough denim trousers she wore, the dry sandwiches for lunch and the propaganda posters that were everywhere. She had hoped to have some word about the Japanese family that ran the produce stand at Jergins' Market, but the only thing she could tell me was they were sent to Santa Anita Race Track and kept there before going onto Manzanar, a detention camp near Bishop on the California desert.

She yearned to feel the softness of velvet on her shoulders again and the cool slickness of nylon hose. This was all she needed as a convincing reason to continue her job and help get the world back on its feet. But she felt an obligation to me also. Then there was Dad who was trying to get on his feet and she hoped to encourage him with all her strength but she could see by his expressionless face, by the tired droop of his shoulders that he was a beaten man. Dividing her time between work and the home was difficult. Eventually she was forced to leave the factory work, but continued with Red Cross volunteer duties.

Dyersburg, Tennessee
June 17th 1943
Dear Folks and Nancy,
Here we are another 48 hour pass, this time in Memphis.
I should have written a lot sooner – but time goes so fast, especially when I don't have any to begin with. My schedule this week is the best. The day begins at 7:30 A.M. and ends at 8:00 P.M
About the weather. We have some gigantic thunderheads. They are as high as 30,000 feet – (6 miles). I have been within 5,000 feet of the top of them. Regardless of what plane I'm in, the sight is impressive.

A few days later, he finished the letter.
June 20th
We are back from the 48 hour pass. My schedule has changed, now it's the grave yard shift. Flying from 1:30 A.M. until 9:00 A.M. then ground school from 10:00 to 2:00. Sleep from? to ??

We have been having a wonderful time considering "Dear" Uncle Sam takes most of my time. So far . . . . Well I guess you know we have moved. The room in the other house wasn't very nice. It was made in the attic which made it very warm. Now we are in a nice house just outside of the "Gathering spot for farmers on Saturday night." The people are very nice to us, they gave us a ride into Memphis during my last pass.

I don't know what you would like to know. I am living (sleeping) off the post since I became a husband. I have a pass that is just like the real one – very convenient. Dorothy Barbara eats most of her meals on the post with me.

I'll write more later.

Love, Bob and D.B.

Constantly on edge, listening to the war news on the radio, Mother tried to keep the home life normal. The routine was always the same. Monday was for changing sheets and washing clothes. Tuesday was ironing and so forth. Sundays were dull and quiet. First the Los Angeles Times would arrive at the door. I grabbed the funny papers and read: *Terry and the Pirates, Dick Tracy* and my favorite, *Brenda Starr, girl reporter*. She had a mystery man who sent her black orchids and had a patch over one eye. Mother read the news of the war in Europe and Dad didn't read anything. He preferred to listen to the radio and if there was a baseball game, he would fall asleep in his chair listening to the plays.

Church was at 11 o'clock followed by the main meal of the day and usually with Aunt Frances or other members of Mother's family. The mid-day meal was often fried rabbit. Since I didn't like chicken, having seen a neighbor boy wring the neck off of one, I would only eat fried rabbit and it was pretty good. Mother spent most of the afternoon arguing with Uncle Harry (her brother-in-law) about the war and when it would end. I played with my dolls or games with my cousins. We all missed Bob and his name always came up in the conversations.

Letters were now coming from Dorothy Barbara and Bob. It didn't really matter who wrote the letter as long as we got the news.

Dyersburg, Tennessee

June 18,

Dear Folks

Hello everybody. Thanks for believing in us, we really haven't forgotten you at all. But Bob seems to be taking up all of my time (am I glad!!!}

Right now my wonderful husband is sound asleep. He should be waiting to take me to the Magnolia Gardens on the roof, for dancing – but he is just worn out. We are on another 48 hour pass in Memphis. Bob and I have been shopping most of the day.

Oh you should see the lovely blue crepe dress he bought for our third week anniversary. You people have a wonderful son. I am so happy with him.

This evening we went to a show (the Lowe's State of all places). We then were coming back to dance – but I just haven't the heart to wake him.

One of these days you will be receiving the letter I am in process of writing which tells all about our start here so far.

Bob had been lucky in being able to come in every night. Also he didn't fly for a couple of days, which made if very nice for me

Very soon the crew will be going on three day missions to the Gulf, Florida and just anywhere. I must tell you – I have moved from Mrs. Irises to the most hospitable home in the south. Mr. & Mrs. Daws on 209 So. Church St.

Mrs. Daws treats me like one of her own daughters. She has three – one married and a most fascinating girl of 19.

Mrs. Daws drove us into Memphis yesterday (My but it seems like we have been here longer than two days).

We won't have to be back until 4:00 tomorrow.

Blossom is still, shall I say "stuck" at Mrs. Irises. But we will have another place for her soon.

We go out to the post twice a day and have dinner about 2:45, then the boys are in class until 8:45 and we meet them again for supper – and home. We cheated the other night, picked them up at 7:30 and went to the show.

Dad by the 5 of us, I meant, Carl, (pilot); Blossom and Tommy (bombardier); Bob and me. (She was answering his question from a previous letter, I presume).

It's too late to go dancing now so I'll start to get ready for bed – although I am not sleepy.

Nancy, here are a couple of the new pennies. Maybe you don't have any yet. Also I am enclosing a pair of wings Bob got for you.

Please tell everyone hello for us.

Mother don't let your career be your main interest, remember us.

Happy Father's Day to you Dad
Good-night

Love, Bob and Dorothy Barbara

We all wished we could be with them. Letters were great but we longed for pictures and more news – news - news. The mailman was very popular at our place and Mother remembered to give him $5.00 at Christmas time. "If everyone gave him $5.00 he would have a nice present," she said.

In a matter of weeks, Bob got his orders. The rumor had been confirmed. The Eighth Air Force would be going to England in less than a month. Tommy having been transferred to another squadron would ship out sooner. Blossom was devastated. She was expecting a baby and hoped that Tommy would be stationed stateside. To cheer themselves D.B. and Blossom decided to give a party. They strung colored crepe paper around the room, pushed the bedroom dresser into the center to use for a serving table and then prepared refreshments using the best of their knowledge and supplies.

At the party Tommy said that he and Blossom had met life long friends here and wanted to invite them all to the ranch they would have someday.

Any time Bob had off was important and he spent every minute of it with his new bride. Day after day the conversations between the crews grew more depressing. Bob did not want to listen but he could not always escape. He did not want to hear about the possibility of death. It seemed to be surrounding him now and he felt the fellows were not helping the situation by talking about it.

Army Air Base
Dyersburg, Tennessee
June 21, 1943
Dear Folks and Nancy,
This is my sixth attempt to write a letter. Time does pass quickly – that's when I have any to myself (ourselves).

So far I have been doing pretty good about getting off the post. Carl was grounded for three days. All I had to do is go to ground school for four hours, the remainder of time was mine. I am afraid that it's not going to be so good for the next two weeks. My schedule has been changed. I fly from 1:30 A.M. to 8:00 A.M. then ground school from 10:00 A.M. until 2:00 P.M. Sleep from? to??

Dorothy Barbara has moved to a new place and what an improvement. We have a small bed room in the front of the house. The people really try to make us feel at home. (Then there is a drawing of the house plan and a lay-out of the base).

It <u>really</u> is <u>hot</u> here. It was 130 degrees at Blythe when I was there, but that's not bad compared to 90-100 here, the relative humidity is almost 100% or in other words there isn't anything like evaporation around here, we just trickle and drip! Say what they may, Southern California is the place to live.

I still feel the same about the army – or flying – or lack of flying. I don't think about it but when I see a picture or hear of a P-38 or A-20 well....

Dorothy Barbara eats most of her meals at the post (except breakfast). She has only had breakfast two or three times since she has been here.

We are going to the show at 5:30 (now it is 5:10) then after that eat and - to bed and try to sleep in this sticky climate. The fan is worth its weight in gold.

About the weather, we have some gigantic thunderheads. They are as high as 30,000 feet (6 miles) I have been within 5,000 feet of the top of them. Regardless of what plane I would be in, the sight is impressive. To be cont'd.....

(Here Dorothy Barbara took over with greetings).

"We don't know how long we will be here, but a bunch of new crews came in last week so it sort of looks like they will be moving soon. Once it was to be the 15th of July.

The fellows have been talking about going home before they go to Kansas, but it will only be six days. Unless Bob can fly both ways it doesn't look as if we would be coming home.

They may change their minds of course, and may give the boys a two week leave. I do hope so.

On the following Friday Bob left on an overnight practice bombing mission to Gulfport, Mississippi. A letter from D.B. reported that he had tried to call but could not get a line through. He was remembering that they had been married for 4 weeks. By Sunday afternoon she had not heard from him and learned his ship had trouble and he had to stay back.

Dyersburg, Tennessee
July 8, 1943

Dearest Folks, Nancy

You must be ready to disown me already. I should have let you know about Bob. He did get home finally.

It was early Wednesday morning (4:30 a.m.) of course we were surprised and pleased.

The very next day Thursday, we had our 48 hour pass and hopped off to Memphis. There was the gay whirl of lights, dancing (yes my darling husband can dance!) In fact the darling is trying hard to become a jitterbug!!!

We went to the Magnolia Roof Garden one night and the Plantation Roof Garden the next. Hm.....

Bob has a much better schedule now. Instead of flying and having Ground School both the same day, he only has one a day now.

The boys aren't as tired at night and we have more waking hours together. He used to be just about dead every night. But he is a grand sport about it.

The other morning I made the best omelet. Bob seemed quite pleased. Twice now I have made breakfast for him and he is still flying high.

One favor I know you will grant. Please could you send detail instructions on how to make an angel pie? Bob said he would like one before he goes over.

Now that brings up a very important problem.

Before Bob goes to Kansas to get his new plane – he will be given a 6 day leave. No longer. Now this won't give him much time since he has to be in Kansas on the 6th day. It seems rather doubtful that he will be able to come to California.

Do you think you might come half way, then you could see him before he goes over?

After the boys arrive in Kansas and take over the new plane – they will take a few practice missions and then the good-bye for a............while.

Say would you try and take some snap shots of the kitty and send them to Bob. We nearly had a wet session (tears) over it last night. He doesn't say much about the kitty, but every time Dad writes about kitty he smiles.

I hope you don't mind a letter from me. I am sure Bob will write soon. We haven't any thing planned for tonight. I'll keep the thought anyway. He does think about writing.

Hello to all the neighbors
Love to you all
Dorothy Barbara
P.S. Bob seems to like the idea of us meeting somewhere

along the line. It would be so nice if we could work it out. Would you suggest the meeting place please?

P.S.S. We can get bobby pins at the P.X. – need some?

XII Laughing on the Outside, Crying on the Inside

> Dyersburg, Tennessee
> *Dear Folks and Nancy*
> *Well ....time flies* (drawing of tiny flies) *as usual. Some of the fellows in the other squadron have been to Salina, Kansas where they picked up some brand new B-17's – so it won't be long before they will take a trip over the ocean. Our squadron comes next. I doubt that I will be sent back to first phase and go thru 1st, 2nd, & 3rd phases as a first pilot. (But who knows?}*
>
> *The Air Corps is being <u>so</u> considerate <u>again.</u> I probably will (or should be) over-joyed with a 6 day leave plus two <u>whole</u> days traveling time before I go to Kansas to get a new plane. S-o-o maybe we could meet you half-way, I don't think I could make it home and back in eight days. Let me know if you could make the trip. This won't be too soon (????) – about three weeks.*
>
> *You know that it will be just a little more than a year that I have been "in". I'll let you know as soon as something definite happens.*
>
> *This is just a note. I'll write you a good long letter before or at the end of this week.*
>
> *Tomorrow I go on a 10 hour flight from Dyersburg (Ten) to Mobile (Alabama), St. Petersburg (Florida) to Memphis (Tenn.) and then home (Tenn.). All we do is set up and turn on the A.F.C.E. or automatic flight control electronics. This flies the plane in a perfect course without any help. Ah! (Drawing of pilot snoozing)*
> *Goodbye*
> *Love, your boy*
> *Bob (Dorathy Barbara's HUSBAND)*

There was not time for Bob and Dorathy Barbara to come all the way home to California before shipping out. A six day leave with 2 day traveling time was all he had, so Mother decided we would meet them in Chicago, Mother's old home town, and have a short visit before Bob went overseas.

Dad bought the tickets and we were to leave from Union Station in downtown Los Angeles around ten at night. It was a big splurge and quite thrilling for me to go by taxi to the depot. Because of the large crowds traveling at this time, timing was at a premium. We heard it was next to impossible to get food on the train, so Aunt Frances packed us a lunch complete with deviled eggs, fresh plums from her tree, deviled ham sandwiches and homemade refrigerator cookies. (Aunt Frances liked to fuss and she must have enjoyed fussing over this lunch). We were loaded with four large cake boxes, tied with string plus our baggage.

The Union Station was only four years old. A handsome Spanish style building with a modern open high-ceiling interior; it served Santa Fe, Southern Pacific and Union Lines and this day it appeared to be serving every body in the world! There were wall to wall people. Servicemen; soldiers, sailors, marines, women, children, old and young were everywhere. There was barely room to turn around. Red Caps (usually black men who carried the luggage) were trying to get through the mobs with armloads of baggage but it was like parting the ocean. No one moved because it was impossible to do so.

It was 10 o'clock at night, already past my bedtime. We waited and waited. Dad shifted his weight from one foot to the other and finally put our suitcases down so we could sit on them.

Shouts of "Hubba! Hubba!" (Meaning anything from "Pretty Girl" to "Get a move on!") were heard around us. We arrived in plenty of time. "Don't worry," Dad kept saying. "We have reservations. We'll make it."

We were still in the foyer trying to get past the gate keeper when the overhead clock showed it was time for departure of our train.

"Women with children in arms first!" the gate keeper shouted several times. "Servicemen in uniform only!" was the next call. Pushing and shoving came from every direction. I was getting squashed. The deviled eggs were getting squashed and beginning to smell badly. Juice from Fanny's plums was leaking out of the cardboard box and running down my arm.

Edging closer to the gate, Dad waved his tickets over his head and shouted, "We have reservations! We've been standing here for an hour, now let us through."

The guard yelled, "Why didn't you say so. Your train is just leaving. If you run maybe you can catch it." He unlatched the chain across the opening.

Running was not Mother's forte especially in high-heeled shoes. (She always wore high heels even in coveralls, probably because she was short). Dad ran ahead down the long dark tunnel. We clopped behind, the drat lunch boxes wagging back and forth from a string. How I wished I could lose those boxes.

We got to the platform in time to see the train pulling out. "There it is! Wait!" Dad hollered. If he had been alone he could have swung himself aboard. But there was no way in the world he could pull me and Mother on after him. "Oh, nuts!" Mother cried. Dad's words were a little stronger. We stood there and hopelessly watched the Union Pacific bound for Chicago pull out of the station without us.

Dad was irrational when he confronted the station master with his views on the inefficiency of the railroad system. He used language that I had never heard before. The station master remained calm. "Well, sir," he said, "you might have caught the train at its next stop in Pasadena but you have stood here arguing so long I doubt that you could make it now."

The Pasadena Freeway had just been built and even though it was quicker than taking surface streets there was a problem getting a taxi and Dad was too embarrassed to even give it a try. So he rushed to the ticket counter and after what seemed an eternity, got our tickets exchanged for the next train out – the next morning.

It was dark and late at night. There was no way we were going to spend the night in the train station sitting on hard wooden benches. But Mother was also concerned about going home. Having put the house up for sale, she had given the key to a real estate company to show the place while we were away. And we had said good-bye to all the neighbors. How embarrassing it would be to tell everyone we were back because we missed the train.

After sending a telegram to Bob and Dorothy Barbara that said we'd be a day late, we went home by street car, not be taxi. No one was on the street car but us. We ate Aunt Fanny's packed lunch for supper. It was a little soggy but anything tastes good when you're hungry.

Thank goodness we didn't have to carry the bags home. Dad checked them in a locker at the station so we were not hindered on our long two block walk from the street car to home. Mother insisted we walk up the dark alley so no one would see us. Then having no key, she shoved me through a dining room window that Dad had pried open with his pocket knife and I ran around and opened the back door. We didn't dare turn on any lights for fear that someone might see it and report burglars.

The next morning we were up with the sunrise, sneaking down the alley. Then it was back on the street car for the nearly one hour ride to the station. We faced the same thing as the day before. Hordes of people shoving and pushing their way to the gate, trying to board the trains. This time Dad took the initiative. He held my hand and pushed and elbowed our way through. The gate keeper tried to tell us to wait, but Dad said, "We missed our train yesterday and we're not going to miss it again!"

The man let us through. We still had to run down the long tunnel, but this time we made it. The Union Pacific sat on the track, steam billowing below its belly. We climbed on board and checked that we were on the right train. Chicago was three days away. Three days with nothing to do but look out the window and watch the dry flat lands go by. I was glad I had brought a doll to keep me occupied. The car was noisy with innumerable children running back and forth, up and down the aisles. The conductor tried to settle the romping herd, but in vain. He ended up stepping over them. The best part of the journey was sleeping in the Pullman car. Mother and I shared a tiny top bunk and didn't move all night. The swaying of the train and the clacking of the wheels on the rails made a lullaby to sleep to.

Chicago was hot and sticky and humid. The train depot was as congested as the one in Los Angeles. We hurried off the train and through the mob stretching to see above the crowd. Bob and Dorothy Barbara were waiting by the gate – a very welcomed sight. Everyone hugged and chattered all at the same time.

Members of Bob's squadron were standing by too, some were waiting for out-bound trains and others to greet their loved ones as Bob and D.B. had just done. Bob made the introductions. Tommy had already shipped out with another group but we met the navigator, bombardier and Carl, the pilot. Much to Bob's relief, Mom was careful not to say she had heard a lot about him – about his absence from the flight line because he was always sick; and how disappointed Bob was to be the co-pilot of the ship instead of the pilot as it didn't seem fair that Carl should be put over him when he never finished his training.

But Dad on the other hand had to say, "I hope you will be careful with the plane and my boy."

"You needn't worry, sir. Don't give it another thought," Carl answered. "He's my right hand man, you know?"

We stayed at the Palmer House, a beautiful hotel with a carpeted lobby and beautiful damask sofas. I was permitted to ride the elevator up and down by myself. The next days were happy ones. Bob gave me a pair of silver wings bent into the shape of a bracelet. A silver chain held it to my wrist. How I loved showing off these pilot wings that my brother earned. We toured the city with Bob and Dorothy Barbara as if we were all on a honeymoon. We rode around on the buses and took a dip in the icy waters of Lake Michigan.

I got to see fire flies, the neat little bugs that lit up at night, so Bob didn't have to send any home in a jar. We laughed about this.

On the last night, Bob and Dorothy Barbara met us for dinner in the Palmer House restaurant. Such an elegant place with finger bowls at each place. This was a special dinner in honor of the bride and groom and somewhat of a last supper for us all. In three days Bob would be leaving for parts unknown. But first he would go to Kansas to pick up a plane so he would ride back with us on the train as far as Grand Island, Nebraska.

The train station in Chicago was more crowded than in Los Angeles. Dad was determined to not be caught off guard this time. When the conductor called, "Servicemen only," Bob went through the gate. Panic set in with the rest of us. Dad was afraid we'd be separated and never find him again. "All others with reservations," came the next call. Dad, Mother, Dorothy Barbara and I were practically stepping on each other's toes. We stayed together until we were safely on the train.

During the trip Bob spent most of his time with Dorothy Barbara but he found time for Dad also, who did a lot of wiping away tears. It was obvious he was terrified he would never see his son again.

"Son, I would give my right arm if you could stay here with Dorothy Barbara," Dad told him.

"Now, Pop, it will be all right. I'll be back before you know it. And you must promise to watch out for Dorothy Barbara."

Dad nodded and blew his nose.

"Do you think you'll stay a few days in Grand Island and visit your childhood days?" Bob asked.

Growing up in Nebraska was another life time ago for Dad. He didn't know anyone in Nebraska any more. "Nope," he said. "We'll take the next train home."

Then Dad asked, "What kind of pilot will Carl make?" Dad asked.

Bob shrugged. "He's only been on one practice mission!"

"That doesn't sound good to me," Dad said.

"Well, this is the army, Mr. Jones," Bob said. "Carl has the intelligence what to do, he just lacks the guts to do it. We all get squeamish at one time or other but Carl actually turns yellow at the sight of the flight schedule. And," Bob paused, "I suppose I should not be telling you this, but it just goes to show you what I'm talking about. Carl told the crew that if anything ever happens to the ship when we're flying, he will not push the panic button. He said it would be better to be captured than to be killed in a jump."

Dad's mouth dropped open. A deep frown furrowed his brow. Bob continued, "But rest assured if Carl doesn't push that button, I will. We're not going down with the ship unless we have to."

A shudder ran through Dad. "Don't say that".

Bob patted Dad on the back. "Don't worry, Pop. It's not going to be necessary. I'll be back."

Dad nodded. I listened silently to this grown-up conversation.

"I don't mind going overseas – except that it's so far away from...." His eyes shifted to where Dorothy Barbara was sitting, head laid back on the seat, asleep. "It's so far away. But it's the price to pay for world peace. Sometimes when I'm up there in the heavens, flying I feel so peaceful and serene – like I'd like to stay right there."

Grand Island depot was small and like all other depots was mobbed with servicemen, mothers, fathers, wives, children, relatives, girlfriends and friends seeing the boys off. Here Bob had to change trains to go onto Kansas where he and the squadron would pick up brand new B-17's and fly them to the east coast. They would probably be the next ones to go overseas. His train arrived with only minutes to spare. Bob had to hop off one train and onto another.

"All aboard!" The conductor called. The train let out a puff of steam.

Dad had tears in his eyes as he hugged his son. "Don't worry, Pop, I'll see you before you can say, 'Jack Robinson.'" Mother could barely speak. She hugged Bob and whispered, "God be with you!" Dorothy Barbara smiled and tried to look brave. I stood behind everyone watching the whole scene, waiting my turn. Bob was leaving; going thousands of miles away to England. Would we ever see him again?

"I'll be home before you know it," he said, blinking back the tears that were forming in his eyes.

"All aboard," the conductor called again, louder this time.

Servicemen all around us gave one last hug and cry of "Goodbye. I'll write," to their sweethearts, wives and families.

Bob was one of the last to board. He squeezed Dorathy Barbara so close I thought she would split open. "I'll always love you," he told her. Then he came to me and said, "Good-bye, Nance. Don't grow up too much while I'm away."

"I will," I said.

"All aboard. Last call."

The train was spilling over with soldiers. Wives, mothers and girlfriends were hanging onto outstretched hands from the windows as if afraid to let go, sensing the sorrow that lie ahead. Bob climbed on at the last minute, as the train began to move, waving from the back steps until he was out of sight. We stood paralyzed watching the train turn a bend leaving puffs of smoke behind. We did not know at that time that he was off to take part in the mightiest aerial battle the world had ever known. My brother, his crew and all the fliers were about to make history in the skies.

No one moved, nor did they speak until the train was clear of the station and they were sure it was on its way and was not coming back. The train rounded a bend and only the high swirls of white smoke stood up. There was heaviness in us all. The smiles and laughter were gone and we had a long way to go home.

Dorathy Barbara looked pale and mother was worried about her. "There's something I didn't tell Bob," she said, "and I hope he forgives me, but I just couldn't do it knowing how close he was to Tommy."

"What is it?" Mom asked.

"Dorathy Barbara reached in her handbag and withdrew an envelope. "It's a letter from Blossom, Tommy's wife. I received it just before we left for Chicago. Tommy was shot down on his first mission. There has been no word from any of the crew."

Dad stared down the tracks that had carried the train away with his only son aboard. He shook his head and shuddered. Mom took his arm and coaxed him forward out of the station. "He'll be back," she comforted. "He will be back."

XIII Off We Go into the Wild Blue Yonder

The Cimarron house sold quickly and we moved back to the duplex on 54th Street. Again the move was for financial reasons. Dad couldn't get a job. Everything he tried failed. He was very frustrated. He even rolled his own cigarettes now.

Mother kept up her volunteer work at the Red Cross, helping in anyway she could. She was extremely patriotic and also liked to keep busy.

> From: Lt. Robert C. Remple
> APO 12290 % Postmaster
> New York, New York
> (On the outside of the envelope is printed these words: CENSORED and then his name).
> *August 13, 43*
> *Dear Mother, Dad and Nancy.*
> *Here I am waiting on the coast to go – where or when I don't know. Since I am not to write about anything about my trip here or what it looks like here or the weather there's not much to write about.* (Following is a 4 inch cut out of the paper).
>
> *Give my greetings to Mary* (girl next door neighbor). *She must feel wonderful. Now with all the men gone she must feel like she is part of the 'woman's world' at home....tsk! tsk! Too bad, just wait until the men return.*
> *This APO number is temporary. I'll send you the permanent one when I am overseas.*
> Love – I am glad I saw you in Chicago
> Bob

Even though there was a shortage of eggs, whenever we got our hands on three or so we made a chocolate cake. Unfortunately grocer's sometimes kept the eggs too long before selling them and they would spoil on the shelf. I was so proud when Mother let me help her make a cake and this one time she let me do it practically single handed. Everything went along smoothly. I cracked the eggs and stirred them into the batter without dropping one piece of egg shell into it. I poured the batter evenly into two greased cake pans and put them in the oven. Then I licked the bowl, as usual. Ugh! It tasted terrible. What had I done wrong? I was devastated. As the batter heated up and began to cook the kitchen did not smell like delicious chocolate cake but like sulphur! We couldn't understand what was wrong until we figured out the eggs were bad. The cake looked perfect. We frosted it, hoping that perhaps the smell or whatever tasted bad was baked away. But the rotten egg smell lingered and we couldn't bear to taste it.

Nothing was ever wasted. Mother passed the cake along to a family who were having a tough time making ends meet. They had four children and the father was out of work. Mother had loaned them some money at a low interest rate to buy a house. A thousand dollars was a considerable sum at the time. They were always grateful and paid her back slowly through the years.

Bob was kept in New York for six weeks which irked Mother. She felt cheated out of the time that he could have spent at home. What she didn't know then was he was being prepared for overseas duty.

(Somewhere in New York)
August 18, 1943
Dear Mother, Dad and Nancy,
I received your letter a few days ago. It was forwarded from Grand Island. I haven't received the razor yet, I don't know what takes so long for mail to reach us.

Well, I'm still here in the U.S. but I might as well be at the North Pole. There are not any public telephones or any way to communicate out of here except by mail. This post isn't like Dyersburg in as much as I can't walk on and off at will.

We are all ready to go, we have been for the last week. We will probably leave on a minutes notice. I sure wish that minute would come. I am so tired of sitting around here doing nothing. It's too bad I couldn't have stayed at Grand Island longer.

I certainly miss Dorothy Barbara. I never realized what a great difference there would be. I do hope you will see her and her mother often.

I suppose you are still moving – or maybe by now you have

finished. It's too bad that Mother can't get some of the sleep I have been getting. Well Dad I hope you get a job where you can give it your best.

It won't be long before Nancy goes back to school. So Nancy hurry up and enjoy your vacation before school starts.

Say hello to Mr. and Mrs. Jergins, Mary, Mildred, Mike and Services – and everybody. (Imagine him thinking about the local grocer, neighbors and gas station attendants).

Love, Bob

(And don't be an old woman about it Dad...thanks).

And then in a separate piece of paper he wrote to his mother asking her to continue praying for him.

Mother;

It looks like I still turn to you when something like this comes along. I am trying to work it out by myself, but I need help.

It's not the immediate dangers that I am afraid of; it seems to be the fear of what I would lose, the loss of the happiness that I have just found.

It wouldn't be so difficult if there weren't so many fellows around – fatalists, ones talking about things they know nothing of and reminders of things obvious that shouldn't be brought to mind. They talk even though I don't care to hear them. They make themselves, everyone conscious of the wrong things. They don't realize what they are doing.

You see it's not only my thought but all of theirs too. If I could only be alone but it can't be that way.

I know you are helping me. (He referred to her continuing prayers).

Love, Bob

While we read his letter, saying that he was waiting on the coast, he was actually on his way across the Atlantic by ship to his destination in England. The planes were flown over by non-combat pilots, many of whom were women. These women pilots could fly anything and often did, transporting planes across country and ocean.

XIV There'll Be Blue Birds Over The White Cliffs of Dover

The gigantic transport ship opened her arms to hundreds of uniformed men. On board, the quarters were cramped with hardly breathing room, but despite of the inconveniences the change of scenery was a welcomed sight to the flyers after days of idleness. Three days out and the newness was worn off. The drills were routine and there was nothing left the ship could offer except the tremendous Atlantic Ocean it was floating on.

The English coast line was sighted one cold foggy morning. Bob was a little excited to be landing finally. Something new and different was waiting for them. Through the dimness he imagined Robin Hood swinging from the trees in Sherwood Forest; Sherlock Holmes discussing a case with Dr. Watson down some dark cobble stoned street and Charles Dickens's Old Curiosity Shop full of books; the Tower of London and the famous London Bridge all loomed up in his thoughts.

The ship docked and no sooner did Bob and the others set foot on English soil, then they were swept up into busses, trucks and any other moving vehicle available and carted off to a small English town on the outskirts of London.

The new living quarters were freshly painted. Bob shared a room with another pilot named, Jack. They looked around at the yellow closet doors, the blue dresser and the ochre colored walls and thought at least it was cheerful.

His first night Bob wrestled and fought with the Sheriff of Nottingham mumbling something in his sleep about protecting Lady Katherine from the villains. When Jack woke him up, he found he was wringing wet with sweat. "Why is it so hot in here?" he inquired. "It seems some joker put too much wood in the stove and it stayed hot."

Letters from overseas took weeks to arrive and sometimes they would come in bunches then nothing for a month. But whenever they did show up it was a pleasurable moment in my parent's life.

How they cherished and looked forward to those moments. Dorothy Barbara was getting most of the letters but she was good enough to share.

2nd Lt Robert C. Remple
September 8, 1943
 England (somewhere)

    Dear Mother, Dad and Nancy,

There's not much to say about the boat trip. You have probably heard what there is of it from Dorothy Barbara, my wife! It was interesting at times, but rather monotonous after the first days. I would like to take another one in peace time it would be a lot of fun.

Last night I walked to a neighboring town. I like it a lot better than anything in the South and the weather is much more enjoyable. The whole town was like one that we have seen in pictures. Buildings built up to the sidewalk or high brick walls lined the streets. The houses, mostly two stories, had low ceilings and very small rooms. All the brass fixtures on the door looked as if they had just been polished. I noticed that many of the door sills were made of a large white stone. These had the appearance of being scrubbed recently and not a foot print on them.

We walked around the town, up and down winding narrow roads with no side walks. Almost every child ran out and asked us, "Got any chewing gum, please?" They weren't as clean as some of the buildings. A cute little boy and girl asked us for gum or American money. One of the fellows with us had some life savers and gave them some. You should have seen the other ones come running, even from blocks away. I just happened to think that some of them didn't know of anything but blackouts and air raid warnings.

All the yards had vegetable gardens. There were cabbage, potatoes, beans – and much more.

The church yard was also a graveyard. The head stones were huge but thin slabs of granite. These were slanting in different directions, weather beaten and covered with moss. The trees were also moss covered.

Their road signs have odd inscriptions on them. Automobiles passing each other on the "wrong" side of the street and funny looking trucks taking up the whole road.

There weren't many people on the streets. Mostly very old people, children or boys not old enough for the army. There were soldiers of the English – or His Majesty's Forces but not even many of them.

I wouldn't want to live here or I guess anywhere else even the States except good old sunny California.

Of course I haven't been around very much but when I get back, I like to compare notes with Mrs. Kanagy (Our neighbor had come from England when she was young) – *maybe these people have changed. With all the restrictions it's rather hard to find something to write about – everything is concerned with the war.*

Sometimes I can see planes flying at high altitudes. The atmosphere is so cold that the exhaust vaporizes leaving a trail like the sky writers smoke. They leave strange patterns circling and diving. These white streaks last for quite awhile, they start in one part of the sky and may end up in another part.

I am just catching on to this money situation, it's as bad as our inches, feet etc. I sent Dorothy Barbara a ten shilling note, that's about two dollars.

It's time for chow. It's very good, better than I expected. The barracks are very nice too. There are two to a room. There are a chest of drawers and a closet for each one of us. The room and fixtures are all painted with different bright colors. Each wing has a different color scheme.

With everything as nice as it is I miss being home, home where ever Dorothy Barbara is. If there were any possible way for her to be here she would be on her way now but —

Say hello to everyone for me. I guess this will be all until next time.

Love, Bob

P.S. I think you can send packages now. I have asked D.B. to send some clothes. I don't know what you are allowed to send but I can use or eat anything you send.

It was obvious that Twinkeltoes missed Bob. The cat really searched for attention. When Mother would come home the cat would stretch out in front of her. Walking around the animal didn't work. Twinkletoes was up quick as a snap and rubbing in and out and between Mother's legs causing her to stumble. She couldn't put her foot down without the cat being right there where she wanted to step. Mother had to run to the door, open and close it before Twinkletoes could get inside. The cat climbed the screen door and cried to be let in. Mother loved the cat too, but there were times for it to be in and times to stay out.

There were days when we all missed the attention we craved, just like the cat, but then we had it much easier than many parts of the world. We read the papers and magazines and saw the newsreels of the terrible bombings over Europe and wondered if Bob was in any of the planes that were up there on the movie screen.

> Letter from Lt. Robert C. Remple (2nd Lt. A. C.)
> 535th Sqdn. BB1st Bomb Gp.
> A.P.O. 634 %Postmaster
> New York, New York
> (Somewhere in England)
> September 18, 1943
> *Dear Folks and Nancy,*
> *I received your letter, Dad. You forgot to put a date on it. I don't know when you had written it. This is the first mail I have received since I have been over here except for all of Dorothy Barbara's letters. Then I got those all at once.*
> *There isn't much to write about. It seems if there is anything interesting to say, I can't write it, its military information.*
> *I have moved since I mailed your "V" mail. This country is really beautiful. Some buildings have thick thatched roofs that look so neat. There are plenty of old boys around the town. What characters, derby hats, boots or puttees, a black coat, a big curved pipe and a big mustache. They just sit around or hobble down the brick sidewalks with their cane. You should see the bay windows (on the houses, not on the men) with their leaded glass window panes. Most of the houses in a section are alike but sometimes they are different, even odd looking places.*
> *It's still the same old army, but I have been treated swell, nothing like it was in the States. Maybe I haven't been here long enough? Well I am satisfied and couldn't be much happier considering I am so far away from my darling wife. Tell her I'll cancel her allotment if I don't get a letter from her very soon and I don't care if it isn't her fault. She should be flown over in a special plane or something.*
> *I never imagined I'd ever be making so much money in all my life. Just think of all the taxes I am going to pay – and all you are paying now. These English people have some real taxes to pay and their wages are low, food prices high. I don't think one of them has complained.*
> *This climate sure agrees with me. Four blankets at night and*

do I sleep. The only trouble is that all my baggage has been delayed and it looks as though I am going to be a bit chilly until it arrives.

It was an unexpected pleasure to receive your letter today. I think of you often, Dorothy Barbara always.

Everything is fine, I'll write again soon.

Love, Bob

The U.S. Post Office brought out a unique little letter designed to reduce weight, called V-Mail. It was microfilmed – a new process – by the censor, and reproduced to its original size when reaching its destination. When sent from the States to England it took two weeks. A very long time when you are waiting to hear from home. We were as disappointed as Bob was that our packages and letters did not reach him sooner. An airmail stamp was 6 cents. The best bargain around at the time and someone in the family wrote every day.

What we were doing at home while he was in England was trying to stay calm. Besides being anxious Mother knew I had to have as normal a childhood as possible under the circumstances. So we joined the Girl Scouts; Mother, as the troop leader and I, as a scout. She did the best she could to keep our troop smiling and help us earn our cooking badge, which was no easy trick with sugar rationing. Mr. Jergins, however was on our side and saved Hershey chocolate bars, Graham crackers and marshmallows so we could make S'mores. Seeing the green uniforms on the scouts brought a smile to his lips and he would gently reach under the counter and bring out treats for the scouts.

As a troop project we rolled bandages for the Red Cross and were awarded a small Red Cross Badge.

(Somewhere in England)
October 7, 1943
Dear Mother, Dad and Nancy,

I have been going to ground school and flying. It's almost like back in Tennessee except the hours are better. The classes are more interesting and so is the flying. I haven't been on an operational mission yet. It has been all practice. If you care to you can read the newspapers, more likely the planes from our field has taken part. But DON'T do it if it makes you worried (meaning you. Pop).

Flying over here is quite different then it is at home. When I go up to high altitudes it gets cold, and I do mean cold. The planes leave a trail of ice crystals which look like sky writing. The fighters do this even more making circular patterns in the air.

I am satisfied with the B-17, especially as time goes on, but sometimes the pilots in these fighters really fly low over the barracks. Then nothing would suit me better than to be in his boots.

I have been disappointed that I haven't met any of the fellows I know that I went to school with. I haven't been off the post yet. I imagine that when I go into town I'll meet some one of them.

I would write more but it's very hard to write about anything.

Would you send Marshall's, Harold's and George's addresses to me? I have lost my little address book. I am going to write to Harold and ask him for the picture of my motorcycle (If Dorothy Barbara reads this say "our" instead of "my"). Tell him that I would really like to have it; it would help my moral – or something.

By the time you receive this letter I imagine the Cardinals will have won the series. I can listen to them playing in the evening, the same time that it is being played. There are a lot of broadcasts I can listen to (a fellow next to me has a radio) if I can be around when it comes on. As you know "Dirty Gerty" broadcasts from Germany and she puts on quite a program. The latest U.S. song hits played by favorite bands are played. I can even pick them up while flying. "Jerry" tries to make us mad at the English and visa versa but it does no harm so we just enjoy their music. It's too bad that the Germans aren't free to listen to our programs.

I have been reading the Bible lesson when I can, at least three times a week and think about it all the time. I know with your help there is nothing to worry about.

Would you and Dorothy Barbara's mother get together and get something nice for my lovely wife. I'll send you some money soon. I'll ask Dorothy Barbara to get something for Nancy. I don't know if I will be able to buy anything for her over here. I would like to and I will try.

If you want to know anything that I can answer please ask me, it will give me something to write about.

Well, I guess that's all for now. I will try to write more often.

I want you to take good care of Dorothy Barbara but don't spoil her. Leave that to me.

I think of you often Dad and Mother – and Nancy, all of you. I'll bet you are growing up to be quite a girl Nancy. It's almost two months since we said good-bye at Grand Island, that isn't such a long time. It has been a long time since I've seen the old cat. I wonder *if she would remember me?*

Say hello to everyone for me. To the ones in the stores across the street and in the apartment house – and Kanagy's and – everyone.

Love, Bob

All the planes had names given by the crew members. Bob's plane was "The Black Widow" and had a painting of the deadly spider on the nose.

England
November 15, 1943 – Monday
Dear Mother, Dad and Nancy,
I could go for some good old California sunshine. I guess I'll have my first white Christmas. Even though it is cold the weather is better than it was in Tennessee but I wouldn't complain if I was there now.

I have the pictures of the old cat. Someone asked me if she was going to have kittens. With such an easy life I guess anyone would get fat. I could also see part of the house, the window with all the coloured (English spelling) glass vases and dishes. (Mother had glass shelves put across the front Bay window so she could display her collection of colored glass objects).

Last week I visited London again. Their subways or undergrounds are quite the thing. I didn't venture on them on my first visit. I thought I would get lost – and I did. They have some double deck busses that I will never go on. They are too high and too narrow. They look as if they might turn over without much effort.

As Dorothy Barbara has probably told you I went through the Tower of London. I saw the very flag pole that Henry VIII used to send the message telling of the execution of one of his wives so that he could legally continue a marriage ceremony with his next wife. No lost time!

There was a display of armored suits and swords. All the fellows in the Air Corps that were there agreed that the armored suits and helmets would make ideal flak suits.

No one may leave or enter the Tower after dark without giving the pass word. Only two people ever know it. The Grand Mayor of London and the King are the two.

Walking down the street I saw soldiers and sailors of almost every nation, no, no Germans. There are Polish officers, French officers, Czechs and others. They are all older men. I guess they wonder about all the kids in American officer's uniforms. We do the job that's one thing they don't wonder about.

I received a package from you yesterday containing two tin cans of food. The way time has been passing it won't be long before Christmas is here. I wish Harry (uncle) *was right about it being over by then, but he would make a better guess if he said it would be over by May of June. Time goes so fast and I have been here for about two months. To look back seems long but one week passes before I know it.*

Everything is alright. I don't have to much time to read (Bob relied on reading the Bible as often as possible for comfort) *but try to see things as they really are which helps very much. There is a Reading Room in Cambridge which I can go to almost any evening.*

One day when I was flying around Ike (one of the crew) *said something about being over Grimsby. I thought I heard of that name before. That was the place where Grandmother stayed when she was over here, wasn't it? I got a good look at it and went on.* (Grimsby was the town in Holland that Grandma visited when she took the Queen Mary to Europe in 1939. She went third class for $98. Cabin class was $224 but that was too much money).

There isn't much to write about (that won't be cut out) *when I am not on a mission, which isn't very often, I have ground school, trainers and lectures from fellows whose experiences might profit us. I also have training flights so you can see I am busy. Then too I go to bed between nine and ten, I never know when I might be called and then it is necessary to have had plenty of rest.*

I sure like to hear from all of you. I know I have hardly written at all but I'll try to write more. I often think about you and what you are doing. I hope you have a good Thanksgiving Day.

Love, Bob

Weeks of flying and classes started over again. Only now the classes were directed toward real targets over Germany. They took practice missions over the English Channel but not over enemy territory.

Besides flying over the white cliffs of Dover and green fields of England, Bob found the flying very different than in the States. High altitude flying above 30,000 feet brought with it a drop in temperature – between minus 40 and minus 55 degrees.

The B-17 Flying Fortress, a 4-engine, long range, heavy bomber – the Queen of planes was what Bob was now definitely assigned to as a co-pilot. This mighty plane could absorb 1000 bullets, fly with no rudder and complete a mission on two engines. It was safe, he told us.

The crews were wakened in the early morning hour while it was still dark and often foggy. They were given a cup of hot tea before reporting to the briefing room. There they got the exact location of their mission before taking off. Scared, but trying to maintain a sense of humor, the crew often told jokes or stories to each other. The story of George 309 became a legend.

"After a raid one ship came back shattered, slashed and in bad condition. The pilot radioed the control tower, "Hello, Lazy Fox. Hello, Lazy Fox. This is G for George 309. Will you give me landing instructions please? Pilot and co-pilot dead, two engines feathered, fire in radio room, vertical stabilizer gone, no flaps, no hydraulics, no brakes, control cables shot away, crew bailed out, bombardier wounded and flying ship. Request landing instructions."

The tower was silent for a few minutes, and then replied, "I hear you, G for George. Here are your instructions. Repeat slowly, please, "Our Father, which art in heaven...."

The news reports at home said that 500 planes from the Eighth Air Force bombed Berlin. All we could think was how mad the Germans would be and retaliate. The papers told us that on August 12, 1943, "Flying Forts batter Rhineland in great daylight raid." Mother knew Bob was in on this. There was no way he sat this one out. She kept a "stiff upper lip" but she was worried about her son. And on August 14th she wished him Happy Birthday, in her heart. He was now 21.

Bob really was a faithful writer and so complete in his reports. He truly loved his family and friends. *"We really had a close one. We were fanned out in battle formation, there were 51's at every hour of the clock, we went into a screaming turn to the right, jacked up rpm's to the firewall and gave her full throttle. Then there was chaos on the radio. "Bogies at 1, 2, 3, 6, o'clock." The ship stopped a hunk of flak and shook, shuddered and bounced as shrapnel tore into the wings, the fuselage and the engines. All of a sudden there was a hissing sound in my ears and I was soon to discover my oxygen was escaping. Man, I thought that was the end. Those lazy black puffs of smoke outside looked harmless but they contained a powerful blow. Let me tell you, that was no picnic. The smell of burnt powder was everywhere and that old plane was trembling from the nose right down to her tail. I was sweating down to my toes. Then in front of us, I saw the crew bale out of their smoking plane and their dirty yellow chutes open and I thanked God they did. All around us planes were going down in red-orange flames. Then by some miracle we were back on the bumpy runway surrounded by fog. Inspite of this place being so cold and damp, I couldn't have been more thrilled had it been New York City!"*

Carl, it seems spent most of the crossing in sick bay but now that he was on dry land again, he surprised everyone by taking charge of the squadron. He was available for every practice mission and showed to be calm and confident at the controls. But his good spirits did not last long. When the first real mission went into effect, it was a different story.

XV As Time Goes By

Lt. Robert C. Remple D-743283
England

December 8, 1943
Dear Mother, Dad and Nancy
I imagine you are surprised to hear from me. It's been a long time.

I would like to see you, Nancy. I guess you have grown quite a bit. How are you doing in school? Do you still go to the same school or would you like to go the Angeles Mesa – that's the one that has the principal you like so much – or am I wrong?

Hey, Dad, what's the idea? You're not going to let me down, are you? I have it all figured out where the women do all the work and bring home all the bacon. You have a good start, now you let Mother quit. How am I going to manage Dorothy Barbara? Now it will be just that much harder for me to carry out my plan.

I hope you like your new job, Dad. I think of all of you and wonder what you are doing.

Remember when we were living on 54th when I was there. Dad would run across the street to Saline's (Bakery) for coffee cake in the mornings. I would like to have some of their cookies or a coconut cream pie but now I have a wife to take care of me when I come home, maybe she will keep me filled.

Sometimes the fog here reminds me of home but it lasts longer. Lately everything has been covered with heavy frost and stays that way almost all day. Its cold but at least I can be comfortable by wearing my winter flying jacket.

Does it seem like I have been here for (approx) three months? It seems so much longer than that. Time does go fast though, its just one week after another. I hope it doesn't take too long before I am on my way back. I doubt whether it will be very soon.

I am kept busy when I am not flying so there isn't much spare time. Then when I do get a little time there are so many personal things I must take care of like washing socks, keeping things clean, laundry etc. etc. It doesn't sound like much but added up it takes time. I haven't been able to read the (Bible) lesson as much as I have. It's too bad that the army doesn't give a certain amount of time for this. It's more useful than anything they can teach us. I have read those two small pamphlets you sent to me. If you come across an article you think I could use, please send it. Sometimes the old devil sure makes it hard to think of the right thing. It seems so confusing at times, it shouldn't be that way. (Bob was interested in the teachings of Christian Science and appreciated reading any literature on the subject sent to him).

    I have seen Norway, Germany, Belgium, Holland and France. That's about all I can tell you. Except for Norway they all look alike. I get an odd sensation when I look down, down where people are living under Nazi rule. I am never afraid but sometimes I know of many places I'd rather be than sitting in the plane. This old mortal world sure tries to be convincing at times.

    Maybe Dorothy Barbara has told you but I am trying to grow a mustache. Go ahead and laugh, everyone else does. It's a contest to see who keeps from shaving first. Its tough going all of us get razzed plenty but I'm not going to be the first one to shave – (O.K. shave what? I know!)

    There are things I'll never forget (in this experience). I'll tell you when I get home.

    I heard a program with Bob Hope as funny as he can be; he knows a few things about what it's like. And its like he said, there are lots of conscientious people that are doing more than their share.

    Say, Nancy I can hear the song, "Any Umbrellas to sell today?" over the radio. Remember when you used to sing that?

    You would be surprised at the things I recall and the things that remind me of them. Songs remind me of more than anything else. The English play some old ones.

    Talking about the English radio programs – the commercial advertising we have is well worth the few good programs we have (or you have). Here there isn't any competition, that American race (?). Even the German broadcasts are dropping off, too bad not much music now. Oh there are plenty of bands – too many.

    The food sure has been good, even if my wife writes telling me of some of the things she has had. Oh, for a big glass of cold milk and a piece of chocolate cake! Or a glass of orange juice. I had two fresh eggs for breakfast this morning! I average about four a month, sometimes six.

As you can see there isn't too much to talk about. I have received lots of packages from D. B., you, D.B.'s mother and grandmother, one from Herman (uncle) and the iron from Mrs. Decker (neighbor). I'll thank them as soon as I can. Oh yes, I got the cards from Frances (aunt).

Say hello to everyone for me until I can say it for myself.

I hope you don't mind relying on hearing about me from the letters from Dorathy Barbara. I will write sooner next time.

Love, Bob

P.S. Your letters aren't subject to censoring – not that it makes much difference.

Bob reported his concern in a letter about Carl, the pilot. Carl was finding the hospital more comfortable than the pilot seat. His ailments were either fictional or brought on by pure fright. He never let the crew know when he wouldn't be there. When a mission was called at midnight, the crew would be ready and waiting for Carl while the rest of the squadron took off without "The BlackWidow" crew who were left on the runway holding their parachutes. They resented this because it put them back in missions and made their stay over seas that much longer. They appointed Bob the spokesman for the crew to deal with the continual absence of their pilot.

(This may be unfair to say about Carl and I'm sure he couldn't help his feelings or he would have changed, for certainly no one wants to be disliked, yet he remained the same character right to the end like a fictitious person in a novel).

Everyone had war fever. Death was near in every neighborhood. The future was only dreams away. "Live for today, for tomorrow may never come," was the motto of the time. Along with everyone else I was getting tired of war and wanted it to end. The Movietone News was full of devastation and sadness. It showed bombed out buildings, homeless people and starving children in European countries. Magazines, newspapers and news reports were only full of bad news.

Mother and Dorathy Barbara and I spent hours together packing boxes with non-perishable foods, mufflers, gloves, warm underwear and anything they could think of to give Bob a taste of home and a little more comfort. Packing for Christmas was the most fun except it had to be done three months ahead of time in order to get overseas by December. This meant that in the Indian summer heat of September we were baking fruit cake and cookies for Christmas. They were placed carefully in air tight tins for freshness. It was difficult to find a small packable artificial Christmas tree and ornaments at that time of the year. Fortunately we were not the only ones getting ready early for the season and Woolworth's caught on fast and stocked all kinds of goodies, in the fall, for the serviceman's Christmas package. Some we marked, Do Not Open Until Christmas. And some said, Open Now.

December 10, 1943
Dear Mother, Dad and Nancy,
I wish I could be home for Christmas or anytime for that matter. It has snowed here and almost every morning everything is covered with frost. (There was some small talk and then he continued). *We flew into heavy flak and smoke. This was the real thing. Everyone held their breath and waited for the bombardier's words, "Bombs away!" Then we could turn around and fly back to England. I saw eight enemy fighters one after another come right at the plane, each one coming so close that I could see the pilots plainly. Each one was opened up, firing, but the plane I was in passed untouched. It doesn't take long for a thing like that to happen but it also doesn't take long to do quite a bit of thinking. I saw my whole life pass before me. It's not the immediate danger that I'm afraid of, it seems to be the fear of what I would lose, the loss of the happiness I have just found.*

I don't want you worrying about me Pop! I don't want to come home and see all your hair gray.

I would like to see you Nancy. I'll bet I won't recognize you you'll be so big. Thanks for the fruit cake and other presents. I wish I could have sent you something from England. I'll send myself someday.

Love, Bob

He said not to worry about him but it wasn't easy after hearing how close he was to being fired upon.

Mother continued to be challenged by cooking chores. Like so many women she got the new fangled pressure cooker. When it started to scream and blow off steam it was time to turn off the gas. But once she missed it and soup covered the entire kitchen walls, floor, ceiling, curtains, windows, tables, chairs, and refrigerator. Food was not important. Getting the war over was.

Sunday, Dec. 18th
Dear Mother, Dad and Nancy,
I am sure that you have enjoyed a very Merry Christmas (with Dorathy Barbara) and maybe a Happy New Year. This mail situation isn't so good. I doubt if this letter arrives before then.

I haven't been flying for quite some time. I was in London from Thursday afternoon to Friday afternoon. There wasn't much to do in that short a time. I was the only officer of the crew to go. Carl is in the hospital with yellow jaundice. I hope I can keep the rest of the crew intact. Usually a crew is split up until the pilot returns.

Thanks for the fruit cake and tin of candy. I gave some of the lollipops and lemon drops to the children of the woman I send my laundry to. She was so glad to get them. She is going to save them for their Christmas.

This winter is certainly different than any I have ever experienced, but I would rather stay in So. Cal. And enjoy milder weather.

My mustache is coming right along – if you look real close. Too bad you can't see it. I almost shaved it off when I went to London.

Everything is well, only I should read more. When something presents itself the more understanding I have – well, you know. As time passes fellows are less conscious of the many unrealities that they seem to be when they first get here.

I'm glad to hear that you are alright Dad – have you new glasses now? (I guess so. These letters take so long).
Love, Bob

At home we were getting ready for Christmas and because of the shortages and the war, I was afraid I wouldn't be getting any presents. The focus was all on the boys overseas. Even Bob's friends were going to get packages from us, but I was not disappointed. The magic skin doll I wanted was hiding in a closet and presented to me on Christmas Eve.

December 23, 1943
England
Dear Dad,
Received your V-mail today Dad. It took over 2 weeks to get here. I'm glad you like your job. When you finish at 3 a.m., I am just getting ready for my noon meal. What are you working on? Parts for what?

I wish I could be home for Christmas too or any time for that matter.

There aren't any thrilling stories to tell. They only thrill I get is when I think of home, D.B. It's ground school, training, lectures, checking the plane, practice flying and missions.

I thought for awhile I was going to have a white Christmas but I guess it won't snow until January or February. It has snowed a little and just about every evening is covered with frost.

It seems strange to be accustomed to flying at high altitudes. I remember one time in Tennessee when I went up to 25,000 feet and thought it was something. I have been above 30,000 feet with temperatures always between 40 degrees C and 55 degrees C. It doesn't take long to get cold if the electrically heated suit goes out.

The cloud formations extend up to tremendous heights making it impossible to fly through. When the sun is at a certain angle it makes huge circular ice crystal rainbows in the clouds.

Most of the time the planes make contrails or vapor trails. A plane can be seen for miles that does this.

I am sure that you have enjoyed a very merry Christmas and happy New Year. This mail situation isn't so good and I doubt if this letter arrives before then (Christmas and New Years). I haven't been flying for quite sometime. I was in London from Thursday afternoon to Friday afternoon. There wasn't much to do in that short a time. I was the only Officer of the crew to go.

There was a long time in between letters, which was difficult for Bob to keep up with our activities and for us to know what and where he was. We tried to image Christmas in England at the Army Base. Would there be singing and laughter? Would there be a turkey dinner? Would there be a decorated tree and gifts? We hoped he was experiencing all that but doubted it.

England
Tuesday, January 4
Dear Mother, Dad and Nancy
I received your letters dated Dec 3rd and 7th last week.

I am sorry that I was so vague about Dorothy Barbara's Christmas present. I didn't know what to suggest and thought that maybe you and her mother would know of something. I can send you any money you need. I hope you did get something for her.

I hope you enjoyed Christmas as I did. I was a bit lonely; I was the only one in my barracks at the time. The large package with all my clothes and the Christmas tree arrived on the 28th. Thanks for the fruit cake and candy and candied fruit. I wish that there was something that I might send home. Things are so scarce that I would have felt ashamed to buy anything. Everyone would know that I was going to send it out of the country.

Our post had a party for about 200 neighboring children. We gave up some of our rations, candy and gum and gave some money to buy toys. I wasn't here Christmas day to drop in on the party. Everyone enjoyed watching the little kids eating ice cream, candy, cookies and cake. They had apples and oranges too.

How did you like Christmas, Nancy. Remember when I wouldn't let you help trim the tree? I guess you can do it as well or better than I.

You should see my mustache. Did you ever think that I would undertake such a thing? I'm not going to shave it off until I set foot on American soil again.

You and I will have to go bicycling when I get home, Nancy. I have a bicycle too. Mine doesn't have any brakes.

Well, I have taken some notes on your letters and I can't read my writing. I have reread your letter and I can't imagine what I was going to say.

I received a letter from Aunt Margaret too. I will write to her soon and thank her for the present she gave D.B. and me.

I am going to a rest home the twelfth of this month. I won't be flying on any missions between now and then. I will be at the rest home for eight days so I won't be flying until the last part of January. The rest home is an estate taken over by the U.S. Army A.C. there are sports; riding, golf, and tennis; good food and plenty of rest. I am looking forward to going. My visit isn't something unusual; everyone goes there once or twice during their tour of operations.

I will be able to catch up on some writing and Bible study reading. I have been neglecting my reading with the excuse of not having time. I do have the time if I really try. I do need the help and comfort that comes from reading. Sometimes I dream of some of the things I have seen and I want to forget every bit of it. It's not the least bit – well – I don't like it.

If things go well I should finish my part of this job around May. I don't mean that it will be over by then because that is very unlikely. The worst is yet to come – the invasion I mean.

I still fill out my clothes although I have lost a little weight lately. Say hello to everyone for me. Well, Pop I wish I could see you *once and awhile.*

Love, Bob

P.S. Please send some cocoa or some hot drink - if you can get some with powdered milk in it. It's hard to get canned milk.

I wrote silly V-mail letters telling him about Twinkeltoes and about my dancing class and anything I could think of. My friend Ruth Christy, who lived across the street and I liked to roller skate around the sidewalk that wrapped around the Methodist Church. (This was the church in which Bob had shot out the windows with a B-B gun. The gun was a gift from his uncle. He was arrested but was let go with the promise to not do it again. Mom had to pick him up at the police station and was very angry at her brother, Marshall for introducing the boy to the dangers of guns). Ruth and I, both around nine years old, pretended to be Sonja Heine, Figure Skater and Olympic Gold Medallist, turned movie star. Ruthy and I would swirl and twirl the best we could on rusty skates and pretend the cement was ice. This is the kind of trivia I wrote about.

XVI American Patrol

England
Monday January 10th
Dear Mother, Dad and Nancy,
Thanks for the long letter, Nancy. I kept unfolding it and unfolding it. I wish I could write a long one like that to you. Now that Christmas and Christmas vacation is over the next thing to come is Easter.

I received your letter dated December the 28th. It sure was nice to know what you did on Christmas, it made me feel a bit lonesome. Christmas Day I was on another base picking up another plane. It was brand new, sparkling but I can't imagine who would want a bomber for a Christmas present.

I don't know how I rate Dorathy Barbara either. I certainly miss my lovely wife, and then to make it worse you tell me how pretty she is. I just get a blank look, staring through the wall and I am 6,000 miles away. Then some B-17 or low flying fighter roars over the barracks and back I come, what's the use. Someday I won't have to daydream.

I sure would like to see Bob Fairchild and the old gang again. I'm glad to hear that he was able to be home for Christmas.

I keep my fingers crossed, hoping that you got something for Dorathy Barbara. What kind of a husband will she think she has who forgets her on Christmas Day?

Don't feel bad about enjoying your luxuries etc. it all comes under the Theory of Relativity. I think the thing that counts is if you realize what you have and appreciate it. We can't conceive how other people live. Even when we drop our bombs I don't think about the people down there, it's just a target and we must hit it. The only thing that "bombs away" means to me is that the mission is half over, I am on my way back.

There isn't much news to write. I am going to the rest home Wednesday for eight week days. I hope the weather clears up and

I will be able to enjoy myself more. I should be able to catch up on my reading.

I have been feeling very good. The weather is miserable – cold, gray, drizzling, windy, etc. etc. I have been wearing overshoes from the time I get up until bed time. I wonder what its like to walk with no overshoes.

I am planning to complete my tour of operations – I don't mean I will be home (necessarily) about May. It may be sooner – or later, but I like to plan on something. I don't believe the war will be over until October or November. We have been discussing the subject. I think we are well informed; we have things to read that the public doesn't know and probably never will. Months pass fast in considering war. Then Japan will be next. What an outlook, oh me!

Ask Harry when he thinks it will be over. I'll bet him my guess will be better than his unless he gives us another six months or more. I don't like to think of what is in store for our troops.

I hope Roosevelt doesn't win again. Oh, well, wait until the time comes.

I think of you often. Say hello to everyone.
Love, Bob

Mom like so many mothers was a collector. She collected trinkets of all sorts. She saved Bob's school notebooks and papers; hand prints from kindergarten, and reports he had made all the way through his school life.

Occasionally she would assort the musty smelling boxes with good intention of throwing some things out, but the memories connecting them were so close to her heart she could not part with them. Flipping through the pages of his drawings it was plain to see that Bob was a natural artist. His printing, learned in drafting class, was even and easy to read and his sketches good enough to frame. In a large envelope was a 9x12 photo showing two pieces of costume jewelry, a bracelet and a brooch, photographed against a black velvet back ground. A note in the lower right hand corner read, "Designed by Robert C. Remple, for Joseff's of Hollywood.

In another envelope was a collection of report cards that told exactly where Bob's interests were. Chemistry – excellent; English – needs improvement; metal art - excellent.

She opened an old candy box containing Boy Scout ribbons and badges, felt emblems taken from high school sweaters, a yard of campaign buttons clipped to a khaki cloth, and other things collected throughout the years by a little boy. There were maps covered with cartoon figures, articles of interest clipped from newspapers, letters to mother and daddy and grandmother in a little child's scribbling, photographs of every class Bob had been in and every brochure sent home from the various schools. She even found a copy of the Follies Bergere program tucked in the back of a notebook.

Near the bottom of a larger box she came across a copy of Life Magazine with a few added loose pages. She thumbed through them. The entire history of the war in pictures was spread out before her. She shuddered. A picture of Mussolini strutting his stuff with a caption of a quote made by President Roosevelt, "The hand that held the dagger has struck it into the back of its neighbor."

Turning the page she found forlorn pictures of the ruins of Dunkerque; the tragedy of ill-fated France and pleas of surrender in Paris. Pictures, pictures, pictures. British women bandaged from legs up, smiling and giving the spirit of 1940 sign – thumbs up. A picture of a widow holding her baby who was chewing on a medal – the Victoria Cross. Pictures of Nazi planes raiding the English Channel – fire, fire, fire – death, death, death.

More pictures of Jehovah Witnesses refusing to salute the American flag and pictures of Boy Scouts with sober little faces, in New York City singing patriotic songs. More pages and more pictures of plane makers working diligently over their drawing boards and on the assembly line. Pictures of planes "our boys are flying"; the T-450, Grumman Fighter; the Curtis P-36; the Douglas B-18; the Boeing B-17 the Curtis P-40; the Douglas B-23; the Consolidated B-24. The B-24 was the Super Fortress fitted with a new type wing. It could fly at 300 mph and it was designed for mass production.

The box held more stuff – maps, pictures of Generals, various kinds of ships, Britishers rehearsing a surprise attack drill, an artists sketch of the liner 'Athenia' sunk at sea by a torpedo "As powers open war at sea," read the caption. Hundreds of people were fighting the turbulent waters while others climbed into lifeboats watching the Liner lie on her starboard side. And then there was a picture of Hitler taken by his girlfriend, Evi Braun. The next pages of the magazine showed Hitler's dive bomber the Junkers 87, a dive bomber developed in the United States. This plane could carry a 550 pound bomb under the pilot and four 110 pounds or smaller bombs in racks under the wings – a very destructive plane.

And at the bottom of the box was a note tied with pink ribbon.

It was written by my birth mother, giving me her love and saying how hard it was to give me up.

Mother showed me this letter and tried to make me understand that I was loved by my birth parents as well as my adopted parents. I didn't question it at the time but always felt like an outsider looking in. She returned the box to the old trunk, closed the door on a world that held happy little boy memories but also a doubtful future and a very confused present.

Five months and five plus bombing missions later, Bob and the crew were sent to a rest home in the English country side for eight days of rest and recuperation. It was an old English mansion, dating back 1000 years, belonging once to Alfred the Great. The estate had beautiful grounds, golf, tennis, riding, badminton, archery, soft ball and good food but no secret panels, according to Bob. *"The bed in my room is so fancy I'm afraid to sleep in it. Maybe someone's ghost has already claimed it."*

(Letter to Dorothy Barbara)
England
Sunday, January 16th
Dear Wife,

"Another day of leisure. After breakfast (fresh eggs, bacon and toast) I played badminton that didn't turn out successfully, the court was damp and slippery. I tried to play catch with a wet football. I got plenty of exercise chasing the ball.

After lunch I decided to look the estate over. Today was an ideal day, typically English. Fog or ground mists were rising from the damp ground filling the glens etc. The building and grounds are beautiful. (Try to find August 16th issue of Life magazine). There are four pages telling about this place. Let me know if you can find it. (You should be able to at some library).

The mansion or whatever it is called dates back to Alfred the Great, over 1000 years ago. Everything is solid oak; some timbers are from sailing vessels. I meant to say that the old boy Alfred lived here. On the ground there is a Burmese Pagoda, given to the owner (R.I.P.) by some trading company. It is beautiful, so exquisitely carved. I am sure becoming antique conscious. The only trouble it's rather expensive. The rug in the main room only is valued at L 15,000 or roughly $60,000. I would like to sneak off with some of the fixtures for souvenirs of course (shame on me for thinking such a thing.)

I have been reading some of your letters over again. You mentioned going to "my" house. I don't have a house any more. (Sniff) I do know what kind of a home I would like. I have been thinking about it quite often.

The letter was continued.

Monday, January 17th

I am disappointed with this place. I have been looking for secret panels and passages without success. Why, any old building like this should have some! I wanted to go down to the catacombs and see where people are buried. Maybe I should ask the sinister butler. If you don't get a letter after this you will know that he has trapped me, probably chained me to a moldy old wall leaving me there. Will I escape if he does?

It has been very foggy outside, the air just drips. Most of the day has been spent listening to records and dreaming and eating. I certainly don't like to leave this place with its good food and soft couches (cushions filled with down – ah what a life!) I dread the thought of the trip back to that muddy post and overgrown tin cans for barracks. I do appreciate it, (I keep telling myself) some fellows eat and sleep in the mud, so I shouldn't complain.

If I stay out in this cold damp climate there won't be a flexible joint in my body. Yesterday I did some exercises and ran about the estate. Now I am paying the price of infrequent exercising. From now on I am going to have cal-a-cent-ics (ah) before going to bed and upon arising in the morning. Of course when it's as cold as it is some mornings I move so much, so fast that I exercise anyway.

I have just found out I have a new commanding officer. It's too bad, the old colonel and I got along together so well. I did like him. I guess it doesn't make much difference though I'll put my missions in as usual. My squadron commander has left too but he finished his tour of operations and by now is on his way home. I would liked to have seen him before he left, maybe could take some of those undeveloped films. (P.S. if, by chance this is censored disregard the last sentence. I was just kidding. Oh yeah!)

It's time to put on my uniform for dinner. It feels so good to lounge around in these civilian clothes. I have a pair of rather bright blue herring bone trousers, a red sweater (wool pull over), and a pair of tennis shoes.

Ah! I am full. What dessert, hot apple pie with whipped cream!

I wonder if you have found the August 16th issue of Life yet. I have been told (I haven't seen it) that it doesn't do the place justice. It shows picnics, fishing and outdoor activities. The buildings are the main attraction. A reporter from the New York Tribune is coming here Friday, the day I will be on my way to the base. I'll try to find out when anything is published. It will be worthwhile to see it.)

Only two more days at this wonderful place. Oh well I won't think about going back until the last moment. I think I will spend the last day in London.

I wish the weather would clear. I could have a few pictures taken, but not in the mist.

Some new fellows came in today. After talking for a little while I found out one of them went to Fairfax (High School). I told him I went to our Alma Mater (Manual Arts High School). He asked if I knew someone named Betty Davis that went there too. He is her husband, Mark Elliot is his name. Small world isn't it. (This was not Betty Davis the actress but Betty Davis who was the Vice-President of the Senior Cabinet in Bob's High School – Manual Arts, located near the Coliseum in Los Angeles). *It was nice talking about familiar things back home – football, Balboa, hamburgers, climate and our wives.*

I think I will take another bubble bath (oh, what a sissy I am). Never let my secret get out – bubble baths tsk tsk, what would the German propagandists say "Brave U. S. Flier takes bubble bath, does he powder his nose? Are they men or do they polish their finger nails?"

Oh, you would never guess who walked in here. I stopped writing and had dinner. I was just about to finish this letter when some new fellows came in. I thought I heard a familiar voice but I have so often I didn't think anything of it. (Now don't you skip any of this to find out who it is). As this person passed the door of the library who do you think it was? (Ah, I know you're waiting for that name. I think I will tell you in tomorrow's letter. I'll have something to write about.)

Now about the weather. It has been rather cold and moist. But I know if you could get a hold of me the atmosphere would be quite different, hot and dry. I guess all this writing hasn't done its job, you probably have skipped this and found out – yes, it was don hilton (small letters so as not to standout). Surprised? So was I! We had so much to talk about. Now its way past bed time so I'll tell you in my next letter what we had to say.

I feel so good meeting someone like him. He is doing fine.

I believe he will finish before I will, quite some time before I. Ten years from now it won't make any difference. I'll be back that's what counts.

Love Bob

(The above letter was written to D.B. and forwarded to Mother. Bob wrote a similar letter home).

England
Tuesday, January 18th
Dear Mother, Dad and Nancy,

I wonder how you're doing with your job, Dad. It's not like the old days at L.A. Furniture. You used to put in a lot of hours there with no overtime. I wonder what we will do after the war. I'm not worried about it. Now I am just letting things come before I start to worry. Everything works out alright anyway.

Mother you would sure enjoy being here. Maybe Dorothy Barbara has told you some things from my letters.

This old estate belonged to Alfred the Great. It has been altered and changed to suit the following owners so there is quite a collection of things in different tastes. The only modern fixtures are in the bath rooms – beds with inner spring mattresses and electricity. There are stain glass windows with the little panes (I thought I was going to say "pain") leaded in. I can't begin to describe it all, the solid oak beams and furniture. Every meal is like sitting down for a banquet – everything is sterling that dates way back. There are carvings, porcelain, tapestries, rugs etc. etc. I'll have to wait until I come home to tell you more about it.

I arise at 8:30 with a cup of hot chocolate waiting for me. Breakfast from 9:00 to 9:30 – ah! What a life.

The weather hasn't been so good which cuts down on some of the activities. Usually there is golfing, riding, badminton, archery, tennis and soft ball – swimming in the bath tubs, that's how big they are.

There are twenty fellows here so it's roomy. I could stay in one room all day without another person passing by. Usually most of us are in the room where the phonograph is. There must be hundreds of popular records.

I have been enjoying myself without doing anything – just lounging around and relaxing on the couch covered with down filled pillows.

Ah! To be a Duke or an Earl or something. (Give me sunny California!!!).

I'll be leaving for the base in a few days; I'll find time to write another letter. Even with life as easy as it is time goes by fast.

I have been reading (the Bible lesson) but not as much as I should, but I guess there isn't any limit of time for that. I do think of the right things and try working things out so I am always conscious of what I am to do. I always think of 'standing porter at the door of my thoughts,' letting only the good and real thoughts enter.

Love, Bob

Don't grow too much Nancy. I won't be able to recognize you. You wouldn't know me either with this mustache. I will shave it off when I set foot on American soil – 'till then. (Signed with a drawing of a mustache).

We all prayed earnestly for Bob's safe return and peace in the world.

Dorathy Barbara went to Washington State to stay with Tommy's wife, Blossom. She had taken the notice of the death of her husband very badly and was expecting a baby any day. Dorothy Barbara was there to offer comfort and moral support to Blossom in this most difficult time.

Washington
Wednesday night
February 2nd
Dear Mother, Dad and Nancy,
Today was quite a day in my life in Washington. Five letters arrived addressed to me. One from each of my mothers and three from my HUSBAND. Oh, I like him so much.

It was wonderful to hear from home, I felt a bit home sick, but I am sure I am doing some good here – so it is better that I am here. Blossom lost it last night after she received word from the government. But she is gaining it back now.

Both Blossom and her mother have told me that they were happy that I had come and insist that I stay until the baby arrives.

Love, Dorathy Barbara Remple

Marshall, Mother's brother, was in the Navy and stationed at the Aleutian Islands. He was a little old to enlist in the Navy but because of his flying experience they took him on. Everyone called him "Pappy," because of his age. He didn't mind. The navy blue and white uniform cleaned him up really well. He even looked handsome enough to get a wife – a tall willowy person with a deep voice and lots of hair piled on her head. She was more thrilled to be a Navy wife than a member of the family. That was certain proof when later on - when he left the service and was just a plain fat man again; she was quick to divorce him.

    He wrote and asked about his favorite nephew often. Bob was always in his thoughts. And now he had a fondness for Dorathy Barbara too. War was in everyone's home and on everyone's mind. Young men – neighbors were dying. It was like waiting for the other shoe to drop.

XVII Gonna Take a Sentimental Journey

Then one day in February a letter and a telegram came at the same time from the War Department. Mother was holding in her hands the letter when I ran into the house yelling something about a used bicycle that I wanted to buy. I stopped dead in my tracks when I saw the scene in the living room Dad sat in his soft winged chair, head bent into his lap, sobbing. On the table next to his chair in an ash tray sat a burning cigarette. Smoke curls gave an eerie look to the quiet, sullen room. Dark, long shadows creased the carpet. Outside the street cars click clacked softly along. The silence of Grandmother's clock tick-tocking was obtrusively noticeable. Someone had forgotten to wind it.

Mother stood beside Dad's chair, a letter falling from her hands. Her eyes were wet with tears and all color had drained from her face. Twinkletoes, Bob's cat was walking along the ledge of the Bay window, meowing as if she knew the dreadful news.

Dear Mrs. Remple,
The records of the War Department show that your son, Second Lieutenant Robert C. Remple, 174283 Air Corps, was reported missing in action in the European Area on 30 January 1944, when the aircraft in which he was a crew member, failed to return from a bombardment mission to Brunswick, Germany."

I couldn't speak. I didn't know what to do. Missing in action didn't mean he was dead. That couldn't be! I couldn't accept that. Bob would show up. He was alive somewhere. He had to be. He was in a plane that could fly with only two engines and could absorb 1000 bullets! He kept saying he would be home! We had to believe that!

The rest of the letter said:
Public Law 490, 77th Congress, as amended, provides that a review and determination of status will be made in the case of each person who has been missing or missing in action for twelve

months. Accordingly, all information concerning your son has been carefully reviewed and considered and an official determination has been made as of 31 January 1945, continuing him in the status of missing in action. The law cited provides that pay and allowance are to be credited to authorized allottees is to be continued during the absence of such person in a missing status.

I fully appreciate your concern and deep interest. You will, without further request on your part, receive immediate notification of any change in your son's status. I regret that the far-flung operations of the present war, the ebb and flow of combat over great distances in isolated areas, and the characteristics of our enemies impose upon some of us this heavy burden of uncertainty with respect to the safety of our loved ones.

Very truly yours,
J.A. Ulio
Major General,
The Adjutant General

Bob's parents were hurting. They wanted to be alone. I went to my room and sat on the bed feeling quite useless and scared. Bob was efficient in everything. He had the respect of everyone. I could see his face right then smiling at me. His sparkling blue eyes hinting of some mischief, his brown hair parted on the side and combed neatly up in front off his wide forehead into a small wave. His cheeks were thin, his nose straight, small ears, a medium build, even though he had at one time lifted weights to be more muscular. Before joining the service he dressed very well in dark blue gabardine slacks and white and blue stripped dress shirts with the sleeves rolled up or blue jeans and white t-shirts for riding his motorcycle. He was only 19 when he left home. I had really only known him for 5 years that I could remember. That wasn't long enough but it was long enough to remember how great he was to me and remembered me in every letter he wrote home.

As I sat on my bed I remembered how handsome he looked in his uniform, how he loved to come home on a weekend pass to eat, talk, catch up with the news and especially to be with Dorathy Barbara. It was always just "hello" and "good-bye" but we loved seeing him and knowing that he was well. Now we wouldn't see him for a long time. Maybe a very long time.

I was embarrassed to face my parents. What could I say to them that would be words of comfort? What could I do? I was the adopted one – not really apart of the family. I felt out of place being alive and well. Bob should be home with his mother and father. Not me. After what seemed like a reasonable amount of time I went to them, smiling and trying to be reassuring. "Maybe it's a mistake. He'll be back. I know he will," I said.

"We have to hope that, don't we," Mother said, bravely.

And then there was Dorothy Barbara. Who was going to tell her? She was in Washington to comfort Blossom, now she was going to be facing her own sad news. Because she was away from home the War Department letter had not reached her yet. So Mother called (uncle) Marshall who was on leave in Seattle and left a message with the operator for him to call back. Mother felt that Dorothy Barbara should be told in person, not by letter or by phone. When Marshall received the message to call the L.A. Operator, his heart dropped because he knew what it was. Something had happened to "Bobby." The call confirmed his fears. Deeply saddened by the news, he could not take the time to even think too much about it. He borrowed a truck from the Navy and drove 40 miles to where Dorathy Barbara was staying with her friend.

When she saw him she was surprised to see him and welcomed him in hoping this was a social call. Then seeing his face, she suspected the news was not good. She picked up her crocheting and twisted the white yarn around the needle, in and out, making the pattern. "I hope I get this finished before the baby arrives." She gave a nervous laugh. As gently as possible, Marshall told her that "Bobby" was reported missing in action. *"She never missed a stitch, but turned pale as a ghost,"* he wrote in a letter. *"She took it like a queen. I stayed about a half hour. She was kind of confused and when I left she was planning to call her mother which seems to be a reasonable reaction as most kids turn to mother at such times."*

In an effort to give comfort, Marshall told her that the military records show that 70% of those shot down over Germany survive. "All things are possible to God." What he didn't tell her but wrote home in a letter was that Bob was in the *"newest, most dangerous job in the world, with 2000, Folke-Wolfes whose sole job is to keep you from getting back to base."* And that the B-17 was really called *"a flying coffin,"* not the safest ship in the skies, and that only half of the bomber crews were expected to make it back.

Dorothy Barbara phoned Mother before she phoned her own mother. Their conversation was optimistic. Neither one wanted to accept the possibility that Bob would be among the 30% that wouldn't make it. As soon as Blossom's baby was born, Dorothy Barbara would be coming home.

She sent a letter.

Hello everyone.....
The bassinet is nearly completed. It does look very pretty and babyish. You would like it Nancy. The baby should arrive any day now.

Nancy, thank you for the valentine. Bob was supposed to send one to Mother and Dad but I guess it didn't arrive in time. Or perhaps it will still come.

I have received two more letters from him. The one written on January 26th, he said he was in the process of being checked out as a 1st pilot because Carl was in the hospital again. "Then I can fly the crew on missions and try to make up for lost time (I hope)."

I intend to write Mrs. Baer (Carl's mother) and see if she has heard any thing. Maybe Bob was 1st pilot – I wonder – so many things. Perhaps Don Hilton will be able to tell us something. All we can do now is pray and wait.

Blossom is getting letters from relatives of the members of the crew Tommy was with. Some of them have received letters from the Government with lists of the crew members and their nearest kin. Blossom failed to receive this list.

We can't help but be brave when we think of how much more others have to endure. There must have been a double reason for my coming to Washington. These people have been wonderful to me. I am a bit homesick though.

I love you all very much,
Dorothy Barbara

My parents tried to be brave, although I could see it was hard for them. Dad lived and breathed for that boy and he was now devastated at the thought of losing him for ever. He had been married before and had two grown daughters, whom he never saw or even talked about. Bob would be the third child that he lost, one way or other.

It was hard to keep the faith when our letters to him were returned with a stamp outside the envelope marked, MISSING IN ACTION. One of mine came back and I was unbelieving. Why didn't they find him and give him his mail?

Then letters that he had written before his last mission started arriving in his voice – hand printed in the artistic way he had. (It was difficult to read them <u>now</u> without getting choked up).

Mother turned into a one woman crusade. Every waking moment of her life was devoted to the war effort. Mornings she rolled strips of sheets for bandages for the Red Cross. In the afternoons she worked as a Gray Lady, volunteering in the Children's Hospital as a nurse. She sewed for the Needlework Guild making things for soldiers or needy persons affected by the war. With Dorothy Barbara and Aunt Frances she packed overseas boxes for the boys away from home. "Bring the Boys Back Home," was the campaign under way. By working this hard, she wasn't thinking about her lost son.

Another letter came from Dorothy Barbara dated February 24th.

Dear Dad,

How's the job Dad? You know they still have "cost plus" here in Seattle. There is some talk of my getting a job here and staying the summer. But I am becoming a bit homesick for all of you.

Aunt Margaret is in Seattle but I wasn't able to see her or Marshall. I'm afraid to leave for fear that the baby will come and I won't be here. I don't know what difference it will make. But after the baby comes I'll try and spend a couple of days in Seattle with them.

Dad, be sure and keep your chin up. There are a lot of people looking to you for support don't let us down, it would be letting Bob down. We mustn't ever do that. He is so strong – let us try and be like him.

Every time I feel like screaming I think of Blossom. She has much more to put up with than we ever will. Yesterday she received the Purple Heart for Tommy. She was able to take it with her head up. I wonder if I could.

Let's just remember how happy Bob made us, and the fun we will all have after the war is over and he comes home again.

We know he has more than many fellows and he will come through alright. He might as well have all of the experiences while he is over there. Each one should make him stronger.

It won't be much longer before we will all be a happy family like we were in Chicago. Then you had better watch out because you will be teased just like we did on the boat.

Love to all, Dorothy (Bob's) Barbara

I had sent him a Valentine so it would get there by February 14th, but it was returned postmarked January 31st.

Mother tried to be cheerful and wrote to Dorothy Barbara: *"Mrs. Jessup received a cable that Dick* (Bob's boyhood friend) *is on his way home. We surely are looking for the day that you can send one like it.*

Don't be surprised if you see a lawn all the way to Catalina Island when you get back because the cadets at Santa Ana Air Corps Base are still paying for grass seed. (Evidently they were replacing the grass on the parade grounds).

Mother corresponded with everyone she could think of for information about those considered "missing in action" and with each answer there was a little more hope.

Excerpts from an article printed in March, 1944 by the American Red Cross – "Prisoners of War Bulletin," by Col. George F. Herbert, A.G.D., Chief, and Casualty Branch.

"The term "missing in action" is used only to indicate that the whereabouts of status of an individual is not immediately known. If a plane fails to reach its destination or another fails to return to its base, - the persons involved can only be reported as missing. When a soldier is so reported, it is not intended to convey the impression that his case is closed; rather, he is placed in this category only until such time as information is secured that is definite and conclusive.

"The brightest side of the picture is occasioned when the individual himself returns to his own company or unit. This has happened in many cases......

"If the missing soldier was a member of the Air Corps aboard a plane at the time he disappeared, the Army Air Forces will furnish the emergency addresses any additional information there may be in his case. This is done without request being made by the family."

The article also said reports would be sent out every three months until they have an answer. So there was hope.

Marshall (uncle) was still in the Navy and wrote on September, 1944.

(Australia)
Lt. J.M. Caulfield
UR-13 Fleet P.O...
San Francisco
Dear Esther, Geo & Nancy, (everyone always remembered me...how nice).

I was very happy to receive your letter it being the first letter I received since I have been here.

The weather is pleasant being cool with lots of showers. It's supposed to get hot about Christmas. I had a very interesting trip down here, although I saw about 99% water. Somewhere along the line a whole day disappeared. (So he must have been near Australia).

We live in a Sea Bee Camp near the airport in tents (not bad really) and have excellent chow. Plenty of chicken, steaks, fresh milk and fruit and good pastry. And I was going to reduce!

We are paid in pounds, florins, shilling and pence. Okay, does that make you appreciate the decimal system?

I am really grateful that John Caulfield (a cousin of Mother's and Marshall's) *is no longer missing and please call Juanita and tell her so.*

I drove a jeep to town down the left side of the street and that's <u>some</u> job after driving for 20 years the other way. Oh, well, Fanny (his sister) *always said I used that side anyway.*

The only thing I would like is the overseas lightweight airmail edition of Life or Time or Newsweek. (Magazines).

Bye and love to all
Marshall

Months later and without official notification of Bob's death, a large box arrived with all his personal belongings – photos, wallet and driver's license, clothes, letters, and his pilot's hat. His Operator's (driver's) license said he was born in 1921; 5'10"; 155 lbs.; blue/green eyes; brown hair. In the wallet was a photograph of Dorothy Barbara, a social security card, pilot's license, and photo of a charter plane like the one he took his first flying lessons in. Also cards with his name and on the back of one the names of his crew members – Baer, Hedin, Norton, Davis, Currian, Cribbs, Pond. It was too much to bear but Mother still would not believe that Bob was dead. He still could be in hiding somewhere. It was not impossible. Stranger things had happened. We had to hold to that thought. We had none other.

XVIII Serenade in Blue

There were promises of peace coming but no real sign. Mother had mixed emotions when 10,000 German prisoners of war were brought to California. In one way she hoped her son was a prisoner in Germany and would be taken care of as well as she knew the Germans would be treated in America. On the other hand, she was angry that they were here and Bob wasn't. Why couldn't there be an equal exchange? Send all the young soldiers home!

Letters to Mother came from Bob's friends without their knowing he was reported missing
.

January 31st, 1944
Aleutian Area
Dear Mrs. Remple,
Only a few minutes ago I received your long letter of January 8th. Now I understand why I was so long without news of you and Bob. By the way my Christmas card to Bob came back to me. No doubt the Postmaster just couldn't catch up with him. He certainly has been getting around in the last few months.
So Bob is in England. I think he's pretty lucky. At least he is in a civilized part of the world and in the same time sees all the action he wants. I have a good friend of mine who just went overseas last December. I have an idea he also went to England. His APO is 9404 New York. By the way if you would send me Bob's address I would like to drop him a few words.
You tell me that your brother flew over much of this part of the country. If so I'm sure he has stopped here often. What does he fly? I mean is it a transport as Army or Navy? I'm asking this for good reasons. Yes, indeed it is very hard to locate a man up here especially if one is not well acquainted with the place and all the outfits on it. I have not yet located Elmer Stokes. One day I was at a certain place where his outfit was working so I asked some of the boys about him. Well it just happened that that day he was off or on

guard duty and I never had a chance to look him up since.

When it comes to weather, the clipping you sent me was very much off the beam. It says that the temperature very seldom goes below freezing. It could have been applied to last winter but certainly not this one. We are not allowed to be specific on the condition of the weather for a period not exceeding one week from the present date. So all I can say is that it's been freezing hard from the past week and it snowed on every one of those days from a gentle snow fall to a hard hitting blizzard. As a matter of fact our hut is completely buried all except for the front door, which is clear only because we shovel the snow away pretty near every day. I have seen many huts that can be reached only through a tunnel. The drifting snows are mostly the cause of all this.

Hardly need I say how much I miss the good old sunshine. But frankly I wouldn't care to trade places with George (Hay) at the present time. Unless it was through a very gradual change. The tropical heat of Panama would either drive me mad or knock me for a loop. I am getting used to this weather by now. But this is far from saying that I like it. I wonder if it will be tough for me when I get back home. I hope I get there during the winter.

I just got through eating supper. We had pork chops and ice cream. Sometimes we eat like kings - I said sometimes. But when it comes to hash, Vienna sausages, synthetic butter, and all dehydrated foods it's a horse of a different color – and taste.

Do you ever see my sister? She still lives above Kelly's place. On second thought, have you ever met her?

Does Bob still own his motorcycle? When I get back home I am going to get me one – if I can afford it. I always did want one but my Dad talked me out of it when I had the money. If I know myself I'll probably break my neck.

Well I hope I haven't bored you with all this chatter. But darn it there is so little to talk about.

Here is wishing you and your family the best wishes.
Ever Sincerely,
Charles Legrand.

Then Charles Legrand wrote that he had not heard about Bob except from his sister who sent a clipping from the newspaper that told of local boys missing in action.

May 1944
Aleutians
Dear Mrs. Remple,

For a long time I had been waiting to hear from you and Bob. That is until recently when I learned from a paper clipping my sister had sent me that Bob was missing. Then it was up to me to write. Believe me I tried, but somehow I just couldn't. Feelings such as these are terribly hard for me to express. So, if I do a bad job of it through this letter please forgive me.

Let me share with you the hopes that Bob is well and safe and no worse then a prisoner of war. As tragic as the words may sound it would be a blessing to know that some day Bob will be back amongst all of you and his friends.

Until that day it will be an honor and my duty to work and fight, not only for my country, but more specifically for the deliverance and freedom of my loved ones and friends such as Bob.

When you hear from Bob, as I feel it will be soon, won't you please let me know so that I also can take part in your gladness and thankfulness.

I remain as ever your friend and Bob's buddy,
Charley

After writing to some of the mother's of crew members, she received answers back but without any new news.

June 6, 1944
Dear Mrs. Remple
Thank you so much for your letter. It was very kind of you to pass on the information you received even though I also received the same letter from the War Department.

Mrs. Polos also wrote to me. She said that her brother wrote to her saying her husband is well but that he is a prisoner of war. Her brother is somewhere in Italy. I am not quite sure if her brother is assuming this or he knows it to be a definite fact.

I wrote to her tonight in regards to this and will be waiting further detail, if you should hear anything more or have any ideas about this please write.

Thank you again for writing and let us hope and pray we will all hear good news soon.
Sincerely,
Betty T. Rigat (NY)

June 11, 1944
Dear Mrs. Remple,

Apparently it is the custom of the War Department to send the next of kin of the missing crew the same letter forms with an enclosed list of crew and names and addresses of next to kin. Such a letter we have received this week.

Some of the other next of kin's have written me and they are as ignorant of the whereabouts of their sons as I am of mine.

If at any time I hear any news that might help you, I shall most gladly send it to you.

All we can do is to patiently hope and pray that some day in the near future we may hear from our boys.

Sincerely,
Louise Van Hise (Mrs. John L.)

Jersey City
Dear Mrs. Remple,
I received your letter and a letter from the War Department the same as you did. I am very sorry I have no other news. Write to Mrs. Sophie Phillipuk and see if she has anything to tell you. I received the telegram on February 12th telling me about the boys missing in action and on February 24th my husband died. Just two weeks later. If you hear of any news good or bad let me know. I hope and pray to God they are all safe.

As ever,
Mrs. Mary Moore

One of Bob's best buddies, George Hay wrote to Mother and Dad saying that Bob was the nearest thing he ever had to a brother.

Cpl George Hay 19102101
Hg & Hg Sq 26 Fighter Command
APO 825 % Postmaster
New Orleans, LA
Nov. 23, 1944
Dear Folks
Hello there, how are you folks these days? I haven't any excuse as to why I haven't written to you sooner except I have been terribly busy. Please forgive me.

Well here it is Thanksgiving Day already, the time sure does fly by for me here. We had a swell diner today, plenty of everything too. I certainly have a lot to be thankful for.

I don't really know how to say this, but I thought sure we would have heard something about Bob. I've talked to several officers and fellows who have been over Germany and have told them about Bob. They all say he most likely is either in hiding or in a prison camp somewhere. One gunner I talked to bailed out over Germany and it took him six months to get back to England. But he said he finally made it okay. He traveled at night and slept in hiding during the day.

Bob is the nearest thing I've ever had to a brother. You know how well we got along. The only serious argument we ever got into was over politics, and neither one of us knew what we were taking about. I often look at the picture I have of him taken by our motorcycles. Gosh but those were the good old days. I just know he'll be back, he has to, and we have so many good times ahead of us.

Well how is everything on the home front these days? All under control I hope. I'll bet Nancy is getting to be quite a big girl by now eh? Tell her hello for me. I hear Marshall is in Australia now. He certainly does get around. Doesn't he?

I had a letter from Wally (Erskin, a buddy) *the other day. He is in Arizona now. The lucky stiff. I don't believe he has been over a thousand miles from home yet. He certainly has had all the breaks.* Dick (Jessup, a buddy) *is still in Florida going to Radio School. He has Jackie* (His wife) *living there near his camp. He says the Florida climate is terrific. From what he says it must be worse than it is here. I told him to have Jackie stay with him as long as he could. It certainly helps one's morale.*

Well here my little daughter will be a year old next month already. You can't possible imagine how much I want to see her. She'll be starting school before I get home if this thing doesn't end soon. I had a heck of a time getting her a little present for Christmas.

I have a 6mm movie camera of my own and have been taking quite a lot of pictures. We'll have lots of fun showing them when I come home. There are some pretty places here, but in general its just jungle.

Well I'll close for now. I hope you both are in the best of health. Tell Mary hello for me to. I'll write more often, I promise.

Bye, bye for now
As ever, George

Mother continued to write and send packages to Bob's friends in the service and they wrote back their thanks.

Aleutian Area

My Dear Friends,

A few days ago I received your Christmas package which it seems had gone all the way up to the Aleutians and back again. I thank you all from the bottom of my heart.

I wish you a Happy New Year and pray that God will bring Bob back amongst you <u>soon</u>.

My sincere wishes and love,
Charley

In April 1944, Roosevelt died and Harry Truman became President. On June 6th, 1944, known as D-Day, the massive invasion of Europe took place. General Eisenhower said they would continue until victory. This was good news and we had high hopes that Bob would be found soon.

Uncle Marshall wrote from the Admiralty Islands

January 26, 1945
Dear Esther and Geo
While the tropical downpour rattles on the tin roof I'll try to write a few lines. Although I have seen many things I always hesitate to write about them lest the censor isn't as enthusiastic as I am. The news from the Philippines is very encouraging. We just heard that Clark Field was captured. That will probably be very significant to us here. I inventoried, packed and shipped some of the boy's things home to their young wives and children. I couldn't help think of the emotions that would be created in all these homes by receipt of such news.

I have picked up several very interesting souvenirs from Leyte including a guerilla gun used by the natives to shoot Japs. The thing is made out of water pipe, in a jungle workshop. It is indeed a collector's item. I also have a printed cloth ribbon of a Jap sailor's hat, picked up on the beach after one of the big battles.

I certainly enjoy Time and Life (magazines). *Especially Time. It's only about two weeks late when it gets here from Hawaii where it is printed. I can't thank you enough for such a swell gift. It's read until it falls apart.*

I trust all the "soldiers of the production line" are able to stand the strain of the war effort. Surely these unsung heroes should get more credit.

I've talked with some army boys who have been out here between 34 and 40 months. Just imagine trying to keep a family together under those circumstances. I think it's a G.D. shame to treat some boys like that and have such ridiculous contrasts in the States.

Gosh, I guess I should write a more cheerful letter rather than airing my feelings.

I am working on a deal to get to the Douglas Aircraft School in a few months, in an effort to split my 18 months overseas in two parts. I hope it works 'cause my little lambkin (daughter) will be a big girl like Nancy before long and I want to see here once in awhile.

Good-bye and give my love to all including Dot. B. Tell her that I remember our nice trip to Victoria about a year ago and what a pleasant companion she was, even if I did have a hard time explaining in Seattle that she was actually my pretty niece and I was not just a rich old playboy!

Marshall

P.S. I received a letter from you just before Christmas mailed in October. Takes nearly 60 days to surface.

We lost one of our transports at a very advanced base the other day when a cub light plane ran into it on take off. 21 were killed including 6 of our boys.

V-E Day (Victory in Europe) didn't come for eleven months but when it did everyone breathed a sigh of relief. Celebrations were on every street corner. The war in Europe was finally over. Most troops would be coming home, others would be sent to the South Pacific.

June 7th, 1945
Cpl. Charles H. Legrand 19099316
3181st Engineer P.D. Co.
Fort Lewis, Wash.
Dear friends,
Undoubtedly you are wondering what ever became of me and why I don't write. Frankly I have no excuse, and worst attempt to make any because I had many opportunities to write. I now even very seldom write home so please don't feel that you have been forgotten alone. Still I was kept very busy ever since we arrived in Claiborne last December. We went there to complete advance training course for general service engineers. Two days after it was over my organization was broken up. The 349th does no more exist. My old company and part of another formed the 3181st Engineer Petroleum Distribution Co. and for the second time we went thru a

whole new and very different eight weeks of training and schooling. We are more commonly known as 'pipe line outfits.' Although it's something rather new to the people at home you may have heard about it. We lay a special pipe line system suitable for field and front line service and invasions and pump gas and fuel to the fronts, air fields or storage depots. I came out of school as a mechanic, that's how I got my Cpl. Rating. We just came back from a seven day bivouac, our final one and will be going overseas very shortly, next week we move to P.O.E. (Port of Embarkation) I wonder for how long we'll be gone this time and where.

Now that victory has come in Europe I wonder if you have been able to receive any news from Bob. I pray with all my heart that you have and that he was safe all this time; for the worst only a prisoner of war in some early freed camp. And I hope that he may be on his horses and journey if not there already. Mr. and Mrs. Remple I can't tell you how sorry I feel for you. It must have been a terrible thing to live all these months in complete darkness of Bob's whereabouts and welfare. It isn't right that the good people should be the ones to suffer so much. It appears to work out that way so often.

It wouldn't be right for me to expect an early answer from you after six months of silence on my part. But if you have any news about Bob, or from him, I wish you would let me know. In the mean time I'll pray that they be only good news bringing your much happiness.

Well I must close now and get ready for retreat. I had hopes of getting another furlough before going over but it doesn't look very prosperous. I hope I get to see you sooner than the last time I shipped out. I wouldn't mind a year too much but twenty-six months would just about finish me up with this Army. Oh well Japan can't last too long, not with the kind of punishment she is taking now.

All my love and very best wishes,
Charley Legrand

A letter from Bob Fairchild on the U.S.S. Wharton USN
Dear Mr. and Mrs. Remple
First of all I want to tell you I am sorry I don't know your new address. I am sure this will get to you though.

I want to thank you so very much for the fruit cake. It has not been eaten as yet. For I am waiting until I am real hungry and want something real good to eat. It is being kept in a nice cool place *where it will not spoil. Thanks again. It was certainly swell of you folks.*

Everything is going along just fine with me. I am afraid though that I won't be seeing Midge (his wife?) *for quite awhile this time. I'm sorry I can't say more.*

I hope so <u>very much</u> that you have heard from Bob by the time this reaches you. If not, I am sure he will be alright. Bob's a good egg.

Well this is about all I am allowed to write so will close thinking about you. If you have a spare minute how about dropping me a line. Ok?

Your friend, Bob Fairchild

XIX My Blue Heaven

In July 1945, President Truman and Prime Minister Churchill presented Japan with an ultimatum to surrender. Suzuki, the Japanese Premier refused the Potsdam declaration as a basis for peace. He was apparently more afraid of the Japanese militarists than of American power. He said the declaration was 'unworthy of notice.'

So on August 6, 1945 a B-29 – Enola Gay dropped a single "A" bomb equal to 20,000 tons of TNT on Hiroshima. Three days later a second bomb was dropped on Nagasaki, killing, injuring and maiming many people. The following day Japan surrendered. It was a decision that many said the U. S. should not have made. Harming innocent people was not the way to end a war. But what no one knew was that the explosion caused fewer Civilian casualties than repeated B-29 bombings of Tokyo would have done. And if the Americans had invaded Japan it would have been a very bloody affair. The Japanese had 5,000 planes with kamikaze trained pilots and two million ground troops ready to fight.

So the war was over. Twelve million servicemen and women were honorably discharged. There were some bomber crews, we learned, that sat out the war incarcerated in neutral countries like Sweden and Switzerland. Dad said they were cowards and if they had stuck it out and helped, maybe more of our boys would have made it home. It was hard not to feel some bitterness. In October, the hunt for Germans committing war crimes began. When found they were hung.

The home front had to adjust to young new families searching for homes and jobs, as well as a gradual increase of food on the grocery shelves. Only now, the small "Mom and Pop" stores were a thing of the past. Jergins' Market was boarded up. Super markets were big on the scene with shelves stacked high for one-stop shopping. Everything was plentiful. Rationing went off and food prices went up. Beefsteak jumped from fifty cents a pound to over a dollar a pound and kept rising. People went wild buying sugar, butter, eggs and products impossible to find during the war.

Still no word from Bob. Even though the Red Cross had no word of him, hope had to continue. Now that the war was over, we would certainly hear that he was in a German prison camp or hiding somewhere in Switzerland. Our hopes soared high again. Any day we would hear the good news.

News came. It was not good. The letter came on a dreary overcast day. Because we moved around so much the letter had gone to the wrong address. It was from the Adjutant General's Office in Washington D.C.

23 December, 1946
Dear Mr. and Mrs. Remple,
I am writing to regretfully inform you that a finding of death has been made in the case of your son, Second Lieutenant Robert C. Remple, 0743283, Air Corps.

The Missing Air Crew Report submitted by the 535th Bombardment Squadron, 381st Bombardment Group reveals that your son was a crew member of a B-17F type aircraft which was lost when returning from a combat mission to Brunswick, Germany on 30 January, 1944. The crew consisted of ten men of which one, the pilot, was reported killed in action and whose body was washed ashore at Great Yarmouth, England and nine, including your son, were carried on the records of the War Department as presumed dead. The fact that the pilot of your son's plane radioed that he was very low on gas and was throwing his guns and other equipment out of the plane in an attempt to make the English coast and the fact that his body was later washed ashore at Great Yarmouth, England indicates that the plane crashed into the North Sea while he was heading for England. Even though the crew may have bailed out, they would have had no chance for survival in the rough and icy waters of the North Sea and the wintry weather prevailing at that time of the year in that vicinity.

In view of the facts stated above and the length of time that has elapsed without any indication of survival it is logical to conclude that your son was killed in action on 30 January 1944 when his plane crashed into the North Sea.

Pursuant to the provisions of Public Law 490, 77th Congress, 7 March 1942 as amended, official reports will now be issued by the War Department which will indicate the actual date of his death as that shown above.

My continued sympathy is with you in the great loss you have sustained.
Sincerely yours,
Edward F. Witsell
Major General
The Adjutant General of the Army

What everyone had dreaded had come about. Dad stopped living at that moment. Mother tried to be brave and she proved herself to be the pillar, the strength that everyone would lean upon. I wondered about Carl, the pilot. Bob had said that Carl was the kind of pilot that wanted to try to land the ship and would not push the alarm button for everyone to jump. Under pressure, I wondered had he pushed the alarm button after all or did Bob do it like he said he would? Or were they all killed before hitting the sea?

The reports came in from pilots and crew of other B-17's. Their statements were all much the same.

The mission was to Brunswick, Germany. While crossing the coast on the way back, the planes were heavily bombarded by flak. An SOS came over the VHF (radio) from the pilot of Bob's plane to "Goonchild Leader," saying they were short of fuel and falling back out of formation. The pilot called for fighter support and began throwing guns and extra equipment out to save fuel. Bob's aircraft never arrived in England. It was presumed the plane attempted to ditch into extremely rough and icy seas of the English Channel but the air-sea rescue boat was unable to find any trace of the plane in the vicinity of the SOS. No parachutes were seen coming from the aircraft.

Three days later the pilot's body was found. No one else. It looked pretty certain that Bob was definitely not coming back. I could not give up wondering where the rest of the crew was. Could they have ditched earlier, or possibly been picked up by the German air and sea rescue and were being held prisoners of war? This was certainly a possibility that I wanted to believe. Or were they all killed before hitting the water? This no one wanted to consider.

Statements made from other officers confirmed the report.

"The aircraft departed Ridgewell, England, on a combat mission to Brunswick, Germany, 30 January 1944. The report indicates that the plane was last seen at approximately 133 hours about five miles off the Netherlands coast over the North Sea, and states that it was lost, or is believed to have been lost, as a result of enemy aircraft. Search was conducted by the Royal Air Force."

Statement of Second Lieutenant Henry Putek, 0804395:

"I was the pilot on B-17G A/C 42-40025 on the mission to Brunswick, Germany on 30 January 1944. While crossing the coast just after the flack was directed at our wing, I heard Lt. Baer call Goonchild Leader for fighter support as he was dropping back in formation. Goonchild did not receive him so he called Dullface Leader, Lt. Ridley. Ridley answered him and Baer again told him that he was dropping back in formation and would like fighter support. Ridley then called Goonchild Leader and told him the story and called Baer again to tell him to contact the leader. Baer did not answer this call or it may be that I could not receive him. That was all I heard over the VHF. My enlisted men saw him losing altitude and dropping back."

Statement of First Lieutenant Bill B. Ridley, 0530079:

"I was Pilot o B-17G A/C No. 42-39906 on the mission to Brunswick, Germany on 30 January 1944. Upon reaching the Dutch Coast on the return route, I received a call over VHF channel "A" from Lt. Baer, who was flying B-17F A/C/ No. 42-30029. He said that he was very low on gasoline, having only about 100 gallons, and was falling back out of formation. At the time he said he was about 3 miles behind formation and I understood him to say that he had four engines running. This was about 1330. At about 1335 he called again, requesting fighter support and I relayed his call to the wing leader, who said he would try and get fighters back to cover him. The last contact I had with Lt. Baer was about 1340 of 1345 and at that time he reported to be throwing his guns, etc. out and said he would be lucky if he made the English coast."

Statement of First Lieutenant Harold F. Henslin, 0741903:

"I was Pilot on B-17G A/C No. 42-31357 on the mission to Brunswick, Germany on 30 January, 1944. Approximately five minutes before crossing the enemy coast of Holland, Lt. Baer started to lag in formation. Shortly after crossing the enemy coast another B-17 pulled up into Lt. Baer's former position. We saw no more of Lt. Baer."

The following is quoted from a photostatic copy of a letter dated 11 June, 1944 which was written by Mrs. Sophie Phillipuk, wife of Staff Sergeant Phillipuk, to Technical Sergeant Vogelgaugh's mother, Mrs. Dora Vogelbaugh of Rock Island Illinois.

"I had some information about the circumstances of the mission from Major Gen. F.L. Anderson of the 8th AAF. I have written to him as he was the one who decorated my husband with the

Distinguished Flying Cross. This is the reply I received from him: 'I have carefully investigated the circumstance in which your husband (this written to Dorathy Barbara) was reported missing in action and learned that his aircraft was returning from an extremely difficult mission over Germany where he had been badly hit by fighters. He was seen leaving the French Coast headed for the English Coast, by other aircraft in the formation. However, his aircraft never arrived in England. In as much as the radio operator on the phone was heard giving SOS's it was quite certain that the plane attempted to 'ditch' in an extremely rough sea. However, the air, sea rescue boat was unable to find any trace of the plane in the vicinity of the location given by the SOS. (<u>Be Brave</u>, I don't like this next sentence either). Three days later the pilot's body was found. In as much as no parachutes were seen coming from the aircraft, only two assumptions can be made. First, that all men were aboard when the aircraft 'ditched' and that all have been lost, or second, there is a possibility that some of the crew members may have been picked up by the German air, sea rescue crews and later reported as prisoners of war."

Dorathy Barbara took the news quietly. She was home now, living alone in her mother's half of a duplex house while her mother was on a trip.

Then came the most difficult moment of all. A package arrived containing two medals awarded to Bob. One was the Air Medal with an Oak Leaf Cluster awarded for five separate bomber combat missions over enemy occupied territory. The citation read, *"...The courage, coolness and skill displayed by this Officer upon these occasions, reflects great credit upon himself and the armed Forces of the United States..."* The second medal was a purple heart dangling from a purple and white ribbon. In the center of the heart was a white silhouette of George Washington. The Purple Heart was given for Military Merit and usually to the wounded or the dead. Now here it was in our hands looking very stern and final. With the Purple Heart came a card from:

    ARMY SERVICE FORCES
    PHILDELPHIA QUATERMASTER DEPOT,
    PHILADELPHIA, PA
    "It is an honor for me to forward the decoration which is being sent to you by direction of The Adjutant General of the Army."
     Roland Walsh
    Brigadier General, USA
    Commanding

A few days after the package arrived, Mother received a phone call from a neighbor of Dorathy Barbara's saying she could smell gas and thought Dorathy Barbara was inside the house. She didn't know what to do.

Mother told her to call the Fire Department and added, "I'll be right there."

I went too – probably because she didn't want to leave me home alone. Not knowing what she would find, Mother made me wait outside. We must have lived closer than the Fire Department because we got there first. The house was locked up tight, all windows were latched and the smell of gas was strong. Fortunately Mother had a key. (I don't know why). She unlocked the door, put a handkerchief over her nose and went inside. I thought she was terribly brave but not surprised. That's the way she was.

Inside she found the oven door open and the gas turned all the way on. No pilot light was lit. Quickly she turned off the gas, opened the kitchen windows and searched the house. All the gas heaters were turned on as well, which she snapped off as she went down the hall and in room to room. Dorathy Barbara was face down on the bed, passed completely out and near death.

An ambulance took her to the hospital, pumped her stomach and saved her life. Or actually the neighbor did by calling Mother and Mother acting without reservation or fear.

Dorathy Barbara did not apologize for her actions. She didn't want to live without Bob. There was nothing to live for. It was not entirely her fault. Suicide was a disease going around among young widowed women and was as catching as measles. Several of Dorathy Barbara's friends had committed the act successfully and died. Perhaps they thought they were showing their sincere love and devotion for their spouse by following them to the grave. Mother gently explained to Dorathy Barbara that she had a long and wonderful life ahead of her. Some day she would marry again and have children. Bob would want her to do this. How brave of this woman to say these things when her own heart was shattered. Bob was her only child. She would never see him again, or his children.

It was a very sad time for all of us. Poor Dad couldn't handle it at all. After that he went through the motions of living but without heart and soul. He died when I was seventeen.

XX No Greater Love

Mother was right about Dorothy Barbara getting married again. After dating several men, she settled on a handsome man, tall and blonde, who had trained pilots during the war. He was very sympathetic to her feelings for her lost husband and understood perfectly the distress she had gone through. Bill Whiteside also loved Mom and Dad and treated me like a little sister. He never tried to take Bob's place, but he certainly filled a vacancy that was there. A peach of a guy, we all loved him maybe even more than Dorothy Barbara did.

In 1952 Mother sold 4 acres of land, near the Los Angeles airport to a land developer for $2000. The land had come her way in trade for one of the houses she and Dad had purchased, remodeled and resold. (After the war there were no jobs for older men, so Dad had to find his own work. Mom and Dad purchased run down houses, fixed them up and resold them for a profit). With the money from the sale of the land, Mother wanted to go to England to visit the War Memorial that the British people were constructing in St. Paul's Cathedral to honor the U. S. Air Force who fought in Europe during WWII. Bob's name was to be on this wall and she wanted to see it.

She took me with her. We went by French Freighter – the M.S. Winnipeg - from San Pedro, California, through the Panama Canal and ended up in Cherbourg, France, a charming port town. A transportation strike was in progress when we landed in France. After one night in a small hotel, overlooking the public toilets, we boarded a rickety old bus, which bounced insultingly over the cobblestone streets, past umpteen bicycles and horse drawn carts, through Normandy where buildings had been left in shambles from the war. Debris littered the countryside. This was eight years after the war and it had still not been cleaned up. The poor people had nothing. Their homes were devastated, fields ruined, cattle destroyed, most of the young men killed. Women and old men were left to do the work and it was slow going. Work was done by hand moving one brick at a time.

Fortunately the Eiffel Tower was not touched by bombs and stood magnificently over the city of Paris. After a few days in Paris we went on to Holland, Belgium and Germany.

In Germany the border guards were still wearing their high leather boots, helmets and carried big guns. I had seen this look in the newsreels as a child and never thought I would see it in person. The guards were big, blonde, handsome and intimidating. They marched into our train compartment and asked to see our papers. Mother handed them over. One looked at my passport picture and then to me. I had no reason to be frightened, after all the war was over. But having been brain-washed from movies and the news all through my growing years and had seen many times how the Germans treated ordinary people, I was not happy to be confronted by this guard in a gray-green uniform.

The guard looked at me again. "Ahh, American! Your photo is dreamlike," he said, handing me my passport and left. I let out my breath.

We crossed over to Denmark followed by Sweden and Norway where we took a Coastal Steamer in and out of the fjords. I think Mother wanted to cover as much ground as she could – perhaps hoping to find out more about her lost son.

One night watching the Northern Lights in Norway, an unusual idea came to me. What if my brother, Bob, was still alive and was on the very boat we were on? There was a man about the age of my brother with a scar across his forehead. I wondered where he got it? My imagination took off and I began to watch him more closely. What if he was my brother? After his plane crashed into the North Sea, maybe he had been washed ashore and was picked up by a family – maybe German or Belgian. What if he had had amnesia for the past eight years and didn't know who he was? Of course he wouldn't recognize me. I was a little girl when he left and now I was nineteen – the same age he was when Pearl Harbor was bombed and the whole thing started. Romantic that I was, the story began to grow in my mind. We would fall in love, neither one knowing that we were sister and brother. It was a story I would write someday.

After 12 days we were back in Bergen, Norway, my imaginary brother left with his family speaking fluently in a language not English. I had been all wrong. But yet I couldn't let it go.

On another ship we crossed the North Sea one night and two days to Scotland, then into Wales, and from there to London and St. Paul's Cathedral to see the tribute to 28,000 Americans who lived and died in Britain's midst during Second World War.

We saw the model of the new altar, not yet built, of the American Memorial Chapel. Mother had the large book opened so she could see Bob's name. There it was – 2nd Lt. Robert C. Remple printed in gold lettering. Mother stared at it for a long time, then finally broke down and cried. We both had to face the fact that he really was gone.

But to this day, I still wonder if he could be alive somewhere!

"Whither shall I go from thy spirit? Or whither shall I flee from thy presence? If I ascend up into heaven, thou art there: if I make my bed in hell, behold, thou art there. If I take the wings of the morning, and dwell in the uttermost parts of the sea; even there shall thy hand lead me, and thy right hand shall hold me." Psalms 139:7-10.

The pleasant and warm memories we all share live on. The kindnesses and goodness that were expressed from this individual live on. A boy that served his country, that gives his earthly life, can not really die, but lives on.

Air Cadet Robert C. Remple

Air Medal with
Oak Leaf Cluster
awarded for courage.
(left)

Purple Heart
awarded for
military merit.
(right)

Notes of Interest

– Balboa Island and Bob's friends. In trying to locate some of Bob's buddies mentioned in his letters, I made a list and with the help of the Internet phone directory I was able to get in touch with one of them - Dick Jessup. He was as surprised as I was. But after 63 years he still remembered me as "the pest." We had a good laugh over that. He remembered the Model A Ford they had and took apart and their Harley-Davidson motorcycles. We talked of Balboa Island, (a man-made island 2.60 miles around located in Newport Beach. The island was built in the early 1900's. Water front property sold for $300 to $500 a lot. Movie stars made the Island popular in the 1930's). Then the most incredible thing happened. In our conversation we talked about where we lived and after hearing that he once lived in a house on Abalone Street on Balboa Island, I told him that I lived on Abalone Street for 10 years - at number 209." There was a dead silence followed by a gasp. "That was my house too!" he said. "No way! Unbelievable!" we both said. He then proceeded to describe the interior of the house and we could not believe that out of 2000 houses on the Island, we lived in the same one; and we had not seen one another since I was 8 years old! What are the odds of that happening? Of course he was there 20 years before I was, but what a fantastic coincidence.

Since that phone conversation we have met for lunch several times. I gave him a copy of this book and he wrote the nicest letter in return. "Sunday afternoon when I got home I sat down to read your book and couldn't stop till I went to bed. Last night I finished it. The letters from Bob were so interesting and so detailed about his training in flight school. I didn't realize how difficult the training was to become a pilot. It was so difficult for your Mom and Dad not knowing for sure if he was safe or not. The end of the book brought tears to my eyes. I know how much the family loved Bob and missed him. I'm glad that your mother saved Dorothy Barbara and that she went onto have a happy marriage. Thanks for writing the book and giving me a copy. Lots of love, Dick."

(His son-in-law also read this book and said he was fascinated with Bob's account of training in the armed forces, as well as what we went through on the home front. He took the book with him to the DMV and while he waited for his appointment continued to read it. And he said tears were streaming down his cheeks and people wondered if he was all right. He had to explain..."good book." Another friend of his with over 4,000 hours flying read this book and commented that he was interested in the program for pilot training during WWII).

In one of our meetings, I remarked that I hoped my brother was seeing us together and Dick assuredly said, "I'm sure he is."

- Pearl Harbor: The attack on Pearl Harbor killed 2,388 Americans and put much of the Pacific fleet out of action. Among the losses was the battleship Arizona, which went down with nearly all hands on board. It is still in the waters of Oahu, Hawaii as a national shrine. The attack came while the Japanese ambassador in Washington was preparing for a diplomatic appointment at the State Department.

After President Roosevelt made a speech to Congress, they responded promptly with a declaration of war against Japan. It followed up on December 11th with retaliatory declarations of war against Germany and Italy.

- Defense Plants: 1941 – Los Angeles and vicinity became the National Capital of defense industries – Northrup, North American, Lockheed, Douglas, Hughes defense plants. Thousands of women went to work riveting planes and welding ships.

- Rosie the Riveter: In the 1930's women worked in proper jobs as housewives, nurses, shop girls or waitresses but when WWII started this changed what was proper for women to do. Posters and billboards advertised for women to "Do the Job <u>He</u> Left Behind." The military called up millions of men, and women stepped into their shoes. They took factory jobs, riveting, welding and all under working conditions far different than they had known before. But they did it with dignity and pride in their work sending battleships and planes to the front lines. Many women joined unions and earned more money then they thought possible. And for the first time in history black women worked side by side with white women earning the same salary. For many women it was the first time for work outside the home. For the first time child care centers were formed to help the working mother. "Rosie the Riveter" became a popular slogan for women in coveralls; and a popular song was written, the words describing the incredible work done by these women.

- The Army Air Corps was established in the mid-1920 and had about 1200 pilots by 1939 the Air Corps increased to 250,000 pilots. By 1944 it reached a maximum strength of 2,386,000 pilots. It was the largest in the world and often called the U.S. Air Force. In 1947 the corps was changed to the United States Air Force as a peacetime force.

- Santa Ana Army Air Base: Construction began on the Santa Ana Army Air Base in October, 1941. The city of Santa Ana leased 1,300 acres and gave it to the United States Government for $1.00 a year. The threat of a West Coast invasion by Japan prompted the opening of the base before it was complete. The first cadets slept in tents. The base consisted of 800 buildings, 18 schools and four theaters. A faculty of more than 250 high school and college teachers was recruited to instruct the future air men. Most of the teachers received a commission in the Air Corps. Approximately 150,000 candidates were selected for air crew training while 30,000 went to schools for ground crews and radio operators. Santa Ana Army Air Corps Base is now OCC – Orange County College and the parade grounds are now the Orange County Fair Grounds. Also Vanguard University, the Costa Mesa Civic Center, and several parks are on the redeveloped land. (I can't drive past it without remembering my brother and the days we visited him on the base).

- Manzanar - 120,000 Japanese were rounded up and detained in camps at Santa Anita Race Track in Arcadia, California. 10,000 of them were sent to Manzanar in Owens Valley. They were kept in one square mile of housing. After the attack on Pearl Harbor, many Americans were afraid that those of Japanese heritage may be spies – especially those on the West Coast. The U. S. Government thought it was necessary for national security to imprison all Japanese including women and children. Most of them had to give up everything they owned. The camps were crowded and several families had to live together. They slept on cots with blankets hung from the ceiling as partitions. They shared bathrooms and showers with others. There was no privacy. Armed guards watched over the camps and no one was allowed to leave without special permission. The children attended school and ironically enough pledged allegiance to the American flag every day. Manzanar, in the California desert was one of these camps and there is a marker today on the site.

- Brenda Starr: Working class women in the 1940's were mostly teachers, waitress or nurses, as stated above, so when the comic strip Brenda Starr, reporter came out, she was an inspiration to housewives who yearned for independence and glamour which the beautiful red-headed journalist provided. And even better, she had a Mystery Man who sent her black orchids all the time. The mystery man had a black patch over one eye and was every woman's fantasy.

- V-mail: In between long letters, we were sending V-mail which was supposed to get to overseas quicker. Some did and some didn't. (V-mail was used outside the United States only to reduce weight. Microfilmed by a censor, the letter was reduced in size and reproduced to its original size upon destination.)

- Trivia: March 26, 1944 postage went from 2 to 3 cents and airmail went up to 8 cents.)
An ad from General Electric in 1942 said, "Fifteen million American men and women are at work today in jobs that did not exist in 1900. These jobs are "test-tube babies," created in the modern research laboratories of industry as a result; millions of people are employed today in welding, in making and selling radios, electric refrigerators, lamp bulbs, automobiles and hundreds of other manufactured products invented with the memory of many now living."

During a recent visit to the Mighty Eighth Air Force Museum in Pooler, Georgia, I learned that my brother's plane was called "Chap's Flying Circus." But all the letters had a Black Widow spider on the envelope.

www.ingramcontent.com/pod-product-compliance
Lightning Source LLC
Chambersburg PA
CBHW020002050426
42450CB00005B/279